A PATHOLOGIST LOO

Natural, Miracul01

A PATHOLOGIST LOOKS AT HEALING

Natural, Miraculous, Spiritual

Dr David Powell

Published by the Powell Charity Trust

Published in 2010 by
the Powell Charity Trust
7 Maes Brynglas, Peniel, Carmarthen, SA32 7HF
Telephone: (01267) 221198
Copies available from this address.

ISBN 978-0-9562336-1-5

*No profit will accrue from this publication.
All receipts will be deposited in
the Powell Charity Trust, and used
solely for Christian mission.*

Printed and bound in Wales by
Dinefwr Press Ltd.
Rawlings Road, Llandybie
Carmarthenshire, SA18 3YD

Contents

Preface

The subject of this brief book has been gestating over many years. During this time it seems to have grown in importance and is the cause of discussion and dissension amongst people of all persuasions. This includes those who profess to be Christians. I offer it as a view written from a medical perspective, realising that there will be many who may disagree with some of its contents.

I am most grateful for those who have helped me in formulating the book for publication. Rev. Dr Edwin C. Lewis has helped me greatly with his meticulous attention to detail. Ven. Dr William Strange was one of those who asked for my views on miraculous healing in the setting of a men's Bible group. He has also made helpful suggestions with the contents. Dr Peter May has been a pattern of clear, Biblical thinking on the issues discussed for many years. He has also generously provided me with some of his own sources and references. Rev. Geoffrey Fewkes has been the source of friendship, fellowship and critical encouragement. I thank Rev. Ronald Clarke for introducing me to Gordon Fee's writings.

I thank those who have read the script looking for errors – Ruth, Gwyneth, Debra and Andrew. The mistakes of fact, script or opinion that remain are my own.

Finally, I thank Mr Emyr Nicholas and Mr Eddie John of Dinefwr Press for their collaboration in publication.

David Powell

Introduction

This book may, at times, be more an exercise in sharing perplexity rather than providing answers. I write it following a lifetime's experience as a pathologist and haematologist, involving the diagnosis and treatment of the living as well as investigation of the dead. This has instilled a strong dose of scepticism in me as to the limits of medicine as well as its contribution to the possibility of the cure of disease and delay of death. It appears sometimes that, as a nation, we regard disease as an aberration which can be abolished by the much publicised advances in modern medicine. The approach to the doctor still has a mixture of an almost superstitious expectancy and an implicit dependence on the achievements of science.

I also write as a Christian. Whilst this is a term that can cover a multitude of sinners, I dislike qualifying adjectives. The church is divided enough as it is without adding further distinctions. I hesitate even to use the term 'evangelical', because this can denote so many differing varieties. It is, however, important to declare my own position at the outset. I believe that true Christianity is essentially a supernatural religion. It is founded on unique miracles – such as creation, incarnation and resurrection. Furthermore, I believe that the Bible is God's word and that, as given, it is true.

It could be argued that these two positions, of a long experience in a scientific discipline and an acceptance of biblical truth are mutually exclusive. Friends have said as much to me. I anticipate there will be few readers who will agree with all I have written. Non-Christians will reject anything savouring of faith in the God who is almighty. Christians of varying hues, whether evangelical, charismatic, reformed, Catholic, or any other, will find something that does not fit with their belief system. However, I believe that any and every Christian should face these issues – preferably before the inevitable crises of human life make them of more pressing concern than a mere abstract discussion.

Christians claim to believe the truth. Whilst this truth is ultimately expressed in Jesus Christ, it would be farcical to deny evident facts when they may appear to be contrary because they may seem to be opposed to our understanding of what the Bible says. This is where I may have to differ from Christian friends whose claims, to me, demand suspension of any critical faculty I have.

Another factor influences this discussion – namely, that of age. I have found in my own experience that issues of health, sickness, disease and death, assume different complexions as one ages. Things that were theoretical become real. As we age, we have to face these issues at first hand, not forgetting that many have to face them at much younger ages. Whilst the Bible should inform and instruct the Christian at any stage of his or her life, we also interpret it differently in differing settings and ages. Even in Medicine, when the young doctor may be able to bring some new technique or treatment to address our illness, there still remains the need for the application of the wisdom which should come with experience.

It is my hope that the non-Christian reader may not be put off by my acceptance of an essentially spiritual and supernatural dimension, because I have tried to be honest and realistic in facing the facts, as far as I know them, in relation to disease. Likewise, the Christian should be able to consider these great issues of human life and be prepared to attempt to reconcile, for example, the claims made for 'faith healing' with the inevitability of disease and death in the life of everyone.

The questions provoked by the claims of miraculous healing are, I believe, of great relevance to Christians. Firstly, they may challenge or confirm the gospel. Subjectively, our faith may be challenged. Objectively, the meaning of salvation and the nature of Christ's atoning work is questioned. Secondly, it has implications for the believer's communion with God – particularly with regard to his or her prayer life.

In places, I refer to real life cases which have informed my attitude. In these I have taken care to make them entirely anonymous and non-identifiable. I have included such cases because I believe that facing actual situations is essential when attempting to reconcile the theoretical with what is real.

In the opening chapters I have sought to paint the medical background because I believe that, despite considerable exposure of medical topics in the media, there remains much misunderstanding. I then try to apply this to our understanding of a Christian approach to questions of disease and healing.

We must also recognise that biblical definitions may differ from modern ideas. The Bible refers to signs and wonders and powers. There may be an overlap between unexpected events that may be explained on a natural basis with those that are completely inexplicable. The fact that an event can be explained on the basis of a well-understood biological or natural mechanism does not exclude the possibility that it occurred as a result of divine response to prayer. It does, however, make any claim as to its supernatural nature subject to alternative explanations.

The Christian believer has no problem in acknowledging that the God of creation has established a world subject to Natural Law. In fact, the inherent rationality of the created order serves to confirm faith. Thus, we see an amazing degree of regularity and predictability in the world. The establishment of Newtonian physics and the amazing scientific advances that have taken place subsequently are, to the atheist, an alternative explanation to the existence of God. To the Christian they are simply a further 'proof', not only that God exists, but also provide a glimpse into the nature of the Godhead. Our God is a God of order.

1.

Who is Normal?

'All the world's queer except thee and me – and thou's a bit queer too.'

When I was a medical student, a prominent Edinburgh paediatrician would repeatedly drum into us that when a mother brought her young child to see us, we should ask the question: 'Is this child ill? If he is not, he is well'. I confess he was the subject of merciless mimicry from irreverent medical students. Undoubtedly, he was teaching us a valuable lesson that we should develop the ability to assess the important question and not miss some life-threatening condition. This should precede any finer diagnostic question. Also, there may be an indefinable aspect to a sick child which is more readily appreciated by an anxious mother than is revealed by any number of tests. The doctor who ignores this is arrogant and dangerous.

This all or none attitude is, however, not necessarily helpful in general medicine and certainly not amongst the older population. The greater the number of medical tests that are performed, the greater the likelihood of finding at least one that is 'abnormal'. This is at the heart of the current tendency in the developed world of medicalising entire populations as a result of the widespread application of screening tests and procedures. We are approaching the time when there will be few adults left who are not taking some pill or other.

The point is that we are all more or less normal. Many biological measurements follow a normal distribution curve (Fig. 1). We describe some people as tall, others as short. We have no

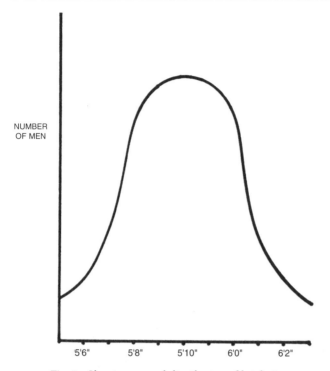

NUMBER
OF MEN

5'6"   5'8"   5'10"   6'0"   6'2"

Fig. 1: *Showing normal distribution of height in a group
of adult men chosen at random.*

difficulty in describing a seven feet man as tall, or one of five as short, but no one can fix on one height as the defined normal. Even if we could, this would vary with gender, age, ethnic and other factors.

In common parlance we hear someone comment that they 'have blood pressure'. Leaving aside the obvious that they would be dead if they did not have a blood pressure, the question is how far from having a 'normal' reading they are. Blood pressure readings in a random population may show a normal distribution curve – although there have been studies which suggest that the curve may be skewed.

How far from some arbitrarily defined normal level does a blood pressure reading need to be, before it is justified to attach a diagnosis of hypertension to the subject? Even if this can be done, we are still left with other variables, such as the accuracy of the reading, the circumstances under which it is taken and so on.

This is a problem which presents in many of our current health promotion schemes. Screening for cancer of the prostate using the prostatic specific antigen test may detect cases of cancer that were unsuspected, but borderline levels inevitably result in men being subjected to further procedures which may carry their own penalty of distress or actual damage. Around 80% of elderly men have been found to have microscopic changes of cancer in their prostates when they have died from unrelated causes. In fact, a number of researchers have argued that the screening campaign for prostate cancer using this test should be abandoned.

Similar problems arise in screening tests for raised cholesterol and lipid levels and the prevention of cardiovascular disease. The number of potential screening tests increases annually. Some of these are sponsored by companies for profit motives.

A touch of cancer?
Quite apart from the problems associated with interpreting quantitative tests, surely there are major killing diseases that can be diagnosed with certainty? Yes, there are. The contrast between a patient dying from widespread cancer and that of a vigorous healthy young person is stark. The one has cancer. The other does not.

This picture is by no means always the case. Cancer may be present without causing any symptoms. The youth, though the picture of health, may yet harbour disease that will inexorably kill him.

There are two aspects and misconceptions to this problem. First, the cancer may be deep-seated and localised before progressing to grow and spread. It may do this with explosive speed and extent, overwhelming the patient within weeks. Secondly, the cancer may be at a stage where its future pattern of behaviour is unpredictable.

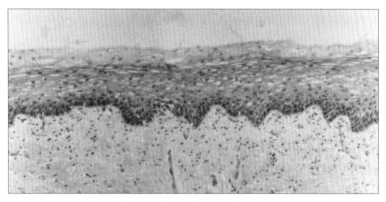

Fig. 2a: *Normal cervical lining.*

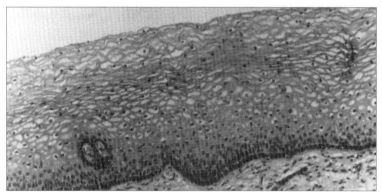

Fig. 2b: *Hyperplasia (overgrowth) of cervical lining.*

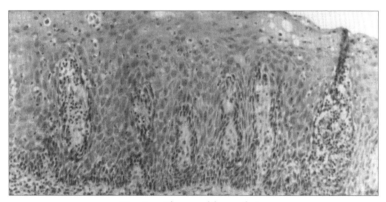

Fig. 2c: *Abnormal hyperplasia.*

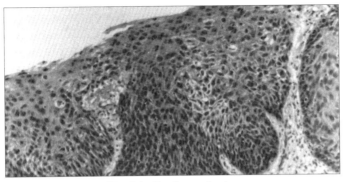

Fig. 2d: *Carcinoma in situ.*

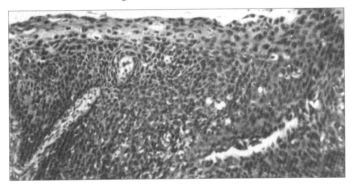

Fig. 2e: *Early invasion of cancer of cervix.*

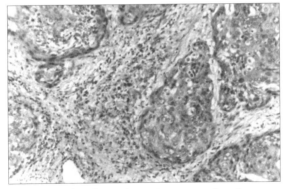

Fig. 2f: *Advanced invasive cancer of cervix.*

Fig. 2: *Series of sections of the cervix showing a gradation from normal to invasive cancer. Examples d-f are from the same patient age 36 years.*

Population screening of women is done for the early detection of cancer of the breast and cervix. The object is to identify cancer in its early stages. In both examples the technique reveals examples of dysplasia and/or carcinoma *in situ*. These are borderline changes (Figs. 2 & 3). The precise nature of these early stages is still disputed, but in general they are taken to indicate that the cells and/or tissues show the changes associated with the very first stages of cancer development, either confined to individual cells or to the most superficial level of the surface of the tissue. The removal of such cells or tissues should then ensure eradication of the cancer.

Undoubtedly, the above argument is sensible and studies have shown its value. However, the benefits can be overstated, because no one can predict the behaviour of what may be latent or incipient cancer in the individual case. When some examples have been left untreated they have been observed to resolve spontaneously or remain unchanged in their original state. It is also often seen that aggressive, life-threatening cancers behave in this fashion from the beginning. The other downside is the unavoidable side-effects of the further investigations and treatment entailed in the attempts to eradicate the suspected cancer.

Misconceptions and misunderstandings

Doctors are often guilty of failing to make allowances for a person's misunderstanding of what is told or written concerning an illness or diagnosis. Perversely, this may be just as prevalent in these days of an overload of information as previously – if not more so. Medicine has its own language and within that its peculiar nuances.

I was at a missionary meeting taken by a man in his late seventies. He was, and is, a wonderful example of a man of a deep, sincere, Christian faith. Some months prior to the meeting I had heard that he had developed leukaemia. He elaborated on this in the meeting, telling us how, as part of a routine annual 'MOT' they had taken his blood sample, as a result of which he was told he had leukaemia. However, he went on to say how he and fellow believers had prayed and he had the promise and belief that he had been cured. When he last saw his doctor he was told he did not need any treatment.

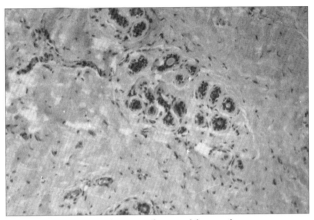

Fig. 3a: *Section of normal breast ducts.*

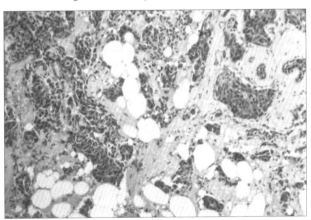

Fig. 3b: *Section of invasive cancer of the breast infiltrating fat and connective tissue.*

Both sections are from a tumour of the breast in a woman of 35. Clinically a small lump had been assumed to be benign. The malignant focus was only 3mm in diameter.

19

It was clear to me that this man had been diagnosed as having chronic lymphocytic leukaemia. In a large percentage of cases the diagnosis is made in elderly persons, as an incidental finding and in the absence of any symptoms, or in the presence of some other unrelated condition. I have seen many such patients in clinical haematological practice. In some instances I would refrain from using the word 'leukaemia' initially when discussing the findings with the patient. This would be criticised as paternalistic in today's climate of full disclosure. However, I remain convinced that the patient should not be told that they have leukaemia without that being heavily qualified. Some of these patients need no treatment. Others may go on to develop progressive disease, but many die of other causes.

I have recently listened to a CD by a well-known Christian songwriter and singer, who told how his world changed, when during a long recording session he stretched his neck and felt some lumps. Blood tests showed the presence of cells suggesting glandular fever (infectious mononucleosis). Eventually a needle biopsy of a lymph node was done. He then received the shattering news from The Veterans Hospital, Texas, that he had chronic lymphocytic leukaemia and furthermore it was incurable. Following this, concentrated prayer was made. He then claimed healing because: 'He was wounded for our iniquities and by His stripes we are healed'. He now claims he has been cured.

This person's knowledge of medicine is as weak as his theology. As explained in the previous case, chronic lymphocytic leukaemia can behave within a very wide range of clinical severity. Although it may be symptomless and not require any specific treatment, the paradox is that it is nearly always incurable. It is not readily appreciated that some of the most indolent and chronic of conditions are the ones that are incurable. The fact that there was accompanying lymph node involvement and a blood picture which was not typical, suggests a form that is more likely to progress and require treatment. Time alone will tell which form he has contracted. In my view, the 53rd chapter of Isaiah is not addressing this question.

Difficulties and Mistakes in Diagnosis

Pathologists are human too!
Unlike the depiction of the infallible pathologist in some popular television films, the pathologist may be mistaken. Errors in diagnostic pathology are broadly of two types. The pathologist may be poorly trained and/or incompetent. A review of his or her work by other pathologists rapidly reveals serious discrepancies. The other category is where the disease itself shows a degree of subtlety that may puzzle or mislead a skilled and experienced pathologist.

A girl in her early teens presented with pain and swelling in her left upper arm. An X-ray showed the presence of a tumour in the lower end of the shaft of the humerus. The orthopaedic surgeon carried out a biopsy of the tumour. When I looked at the slides prepared from the biopsy, I was puzzled. There were features of a malignant growth resembling an osteogenic sarcoma. If this were the case treatment would entail amputation. I sent the slides to a panel of experts who concluded this was indeed a malignant tumour. However, by the time I had received this report, I had had further opinion that the lesion was benign. After much agonising the decision was finally taken by the surgeon that he would carry out local removal of the tumour and replace it with a bone graft. The resected specimen showed quite clearly that the lesion was that of an aneurysmal bone cyst – a non-malignant condition. The patient recovered fully with completely normal function.

Similar diagnostic difficulties may be seen in lymph node tumours and soft tissue tumours in general.

A woman of 51 years presented with a lump in her left breast. Mammography confirmed the presence of a tumour. The lump was excised. The sections showed a 2 cm nodule inside which was a filarial nematode (a form of tropical/Mediterranean worm). The only possible contact source was a holiday in Greece two years previously when the patient remembered seeing 'mangy' cats prowling around tables at which food was taken.[1]

I hasten to add that the above was a highly unusual case, but I include it because miraculous healing is also, at its least, unusual.

This problem has been highlighted in some public health screening programmes, where the diagnostic problem results from a failure to appreciate the range of normality as mentioned above. There have been several over-publicised instances of so-called scandals where cases of cancer have been missed. Some of these have been examples of incompetence on the part of the cytologist or pathologist. There have been a number of cases of women who have had repeated negative cervical smear tests over a period of several years but were still to die from cervical cancer. But probably the majority related to a failure to appreciate the subjective nature of the changes that are found in the cells in early or borderline cases. Careers have been destroyed following headlines in the media of 'scandal', or 'cancer test blunders', accompanied with understandably shocked reactions from patients as they are recalled. Much less emphasis is placed on the fallibility of the tests at the time of recommending them on a population basis. This is especially the case in a country where Government is increasingly disposed to take control of our lives and health issues.

There is also a failure to recognise the harmful effects of the pathologist 'playing safe' by being over-zealous in interpreting borderline changes, with the result that the patient is unnecessarily

1. Ashford, R. W., Dowse, J. A., Rogers, W. N., and D. E. B. Powell, 'Dirofilariasis of the Breast'. *Lancet*, 1989, 1:1198.

alarmed and over-treated. This may not be a major issue in early cancer of the cervix, but can be devastating, for example, if the breast should be removed when early changes have been misinterpreted.

For as long as the interpretation of abnormalities in smears of cells or sections of tissue is carried out by humans, there is always the danger of human error – in fact, some of it is inevitable. Furthermore, the various techniques of automation or quantitative methods that may be adopted to banish human error, introduce problems of their own.

A matter of opinion
In the context of our considerations of healing, we not only have to consider common misconceptions as to the nature and pattern of disease, but it is also vital that we have accurate diagnosis.

As we shall see later many of the anecdotal accounts of miraculous or unexplained healing are based on cases where there is at least an element of doubt as to the diagnosis. Apart from this there is also the possible fallibility of any human opinion.

In the case of the majority of established cancer growths a trained and experienced pathologist should be able to look down the microscope and make the diagnosis without difficulty. Nevertheless, there are a significant number of exceptions.

Some malignant growths may be, as a group, notoriously difficult to diagnose on a uniform basis. Even their names and classifications are subject to changes in fashion, depending on the most recent advances. This is exemplified in lymph node and bone malignancies. In my own experience I recall individual cases where I would refer slides to an expert or a panel of experts, only to receive diametrically opposed opinions, as in the case of the benign bone cyst above.

There are conditions where, as a result of infection or other irritation, the tissues respond by producing an overgrowth that mimics cancer so closely as to be almost indistinguishable. This can be seen with bony growth following injury or infection.

Tuberculosis of the larynx can result in similar appearances to those of cancer.

How malignant?

Another misconception is that the larger the tumour the more malignant it is. The larger tumour may present greater technical difficulty in its removal. But this does not mean it is more aggressive. In fact, the converse may well be the case. The larger the tumour the more likely it is to have been one that has grown slowly, whereas the smaller tumours may be highly invasive and already have spread to other organs before diagnosis.

Is anyone normal?

A pathologist would be either inefficient or incompetent, if, having carried out a post-mortem on a middle-aged man; he found no 'abnormality'. There are always some signs of disease or 'wear and tear', in the form of streaks of atheroma on the aorta, coronary arteries; changes in the tissues of kidneys and other organs; signs of old or recent inflammation on sites of the skin, mouth or lungs and so on. The body is in a constant state of growth, replacement and repair – processes which often cannot be distinguished from disease.

The cynical approach for the pathologist confronting a case of sudden death from an unknown cause, would be to act on the principle of the Scotsman, or native of Cardiganshire, who having lost some coins and looked in every pocket but the last, is afraid to look in that place lest he draw a blank there also. So the pathologist examines every organ, leaving the heart and coronary arteries to the very last, because he has a good chance of finding some degree of coronary atheroma where all else has failed!

For all the above reasons, I would plead for both reticence and rigour in approaching claims of miraculous healing. The diagnosis may be mistaken, misunderstood or misinterpreted.

2.

The Unpredictability of Prognosis

How long do I have?

Anyone confronted with the diagnosis of a life-threatening disease in themselves or in the case of a friend or loved one, inevitably questions when death can be expected. Undoubtedly, in many cases it is possible to gauge whether it is imminent within hours or days, as opposed to an expectation of months or years. It can also be argued that it may be part of the attending doctor's duty to give an opinion on life-expectancy.

However, the giving of a prognosis is fraught with danger – there are so many examples of disease progression behaving unpredictably. This may occur in both directions, when the patient defies all predictions and long outlives his prognosis, or even the prognosticator. Alternatively, the disease may suddenly become more aggressive and kill the patient in a much shorter time. For this reason I believe that the doctor should engage in studied ambiguity on the issue. It is little short of cruel to tell a patient or relative that someone 'has four months', for example, when no one can define such an interval when it could readily take three or five months or a much wider spread of time before death ensues. Some cancers are notoriously unpredictable in this respect. Breast cancer may be treated apparently successfully, only to recur 20 or more years later. In such instances it is arguable whether it is a recurrence of the original growth or a completely new growth.

This unpredictability of prognosis may apply in non-malignant, chronic conditions. *Sky News* on 23rd November 2009 reported on the case of an engineering student who was left in a Persistent

Vegetative State for 23 years following a car crash. He was totally paralysed and non-communicative. Dr Steven Laureyx, Head of the Coma Science Group of the University of Liege, Belgium, investigated the patient, now 46 years old, and enabled him to tap out a computerised message and read from a special device. The patient said: *'I screamed but there was nothing to hear . . . All the time I literally dreamed of a better life. Frustration is too small a word to describe what I felt. I shall never forget the day when they discovered what was truly wrong with me – it was my second birth. I want to read, talk with my friends via the computer and enjoy life now people know I am not dead.'* Such an extraordinary case is by no means unique. It shows how mistaken diagnoses and prognoses happen. There is also no hint of any supernatural or miraculous element.

This aspect of the variability in the progress of a disease is obviously one that must be acknowledged in any consideration of healing or cure, whether from conventional medicine or alternative claims.

Natural Remission
Not only do cancers grow at variable rates, even when they are of the same type and diagnosis, but there are also examples of their complete disappearance, without medical intervention.

Case of John. This was a lad of 10 years of age. He was referred to me because he was pale, tired and had symptoms of bruising and bleeding. His blood examination showed he was severely anaemic, with low platelet count and raised white cell count. The white cells showed all the primitive features associated with the lymphoblastic cells of acute leukaemia. The blood was also tested for glandular fever with negative results. Then a bone marrow examination was done, which confirmed the presence of acute lymphoblastic leukaemia.

He was referred to the local teaching hospital Paediatric Leukaemia Unit.

All this occurred some 50 years ago. John was discharged home on a course of steroids which was all that was then available. They were given for symptomatic relief. The steroids were discontinued when it was expected that the leukaemia would inevitably progress. However, all the symptoms abated. The blood picture returned to normal. I heard approximately 20 years later that he remained fit and well. There was no history of any claim of any miraculous cure or faith healing.

This story is highly exceptional. In fact, it is unique in my own experience of seeing many patients of all ages who suffered from leukaemia. This is why it is so firmly etched in my memory. A critic could fairly claim that in this case there was the real possibility of some disease, such as a viral infection, that produced leukaemoid changes that were indistinguishable from acute leukaemia.

There are more numerous examples of solid cancer, where patients have undergone partial, palliative surgery for cancers of the stomach, bowel or breast, where it was expected that the disease would resume its relentless progress, only for it to confound all expectations.

The *Daily Telegraph* of 5th April 1989 reported the case of a 54-year-old man who had cancer of the stomach which had spread to the liver. The tumour was described as 'huge'. He was given months to live. Then it mysteriously disappeared. The patient said: 'I'm not a religious person and I think I'm pretty level-headed, but if this is not a miracle, what is?'

Then there are those malignancies where endocrine influences may have a major role, although the growth is highly aggressive – for example, choriocarcinoma – a disease where tissue resembling the placenta becomes malignant and highly invasive. This is a condition which used to be highly lethal but is now responsive to intensive chemotherapy. However, prior to these advances in treatment, unpredictable remissions were recorded. T. C. Everson and W. H. Cole[1] described 176 cases of cancer which showed

1. Everson, T. C. and Cole, W. H., *Spontaneous Regression of Cancer*. Philadelphia. 1966.

spontaneous regression. More than half of these were of one of four categories – neuroblastoma, carcinoma of the kidney, choriocarcinoma and malignant melanoma. None of these regressions of highly malignant cancers were claimed to have been the result of Christian prayer or supernatural intervention.

The variability in the behaviour of usually lethal diseases should cause us to approach dramatic claims with caution. Just as in life events, disease may have a highly unpredictable element.

3.

What is Disease?

'There are no diseases, only sick people.'
Hans Selye.

The terms illness and disease are related but distinct, although we often use them interchangeably.

A person may believe he or she is not well. The person is not at ease and therefore it may be thought an expression of a specific disease. Exhaustive testing may fail to show the presence of any organic disorder or pathological condition.

Alternatively, someone may feel fit and healthy (and happy), and yet be found to be harbouring some serious disease. Doctors of my generation, and especially of my own speciality, are trained to look for organic disease as entities. Part of the fascination of Medicine is precisely in this field. The disease is the villain or criminal and it is the doctor's role to identify him. It then becomes a triumph to name the criminal and the rarer or more esoteric the name the better.

The core duties of a surgical histopathologist involve looking at trays of slides through the microscope and then issuing a report with a diagnosis. This may involve twenty or more patients. The diagnoses vary from the banal skin wart to a highly malignant cancer. The pathologist will at times be positively excited when a rare condition is identified – perhaps this is why some pathologists I have known have been keen bird 'twitchers'. This process contrasts with the devastation which the receipt of the report may give rise to as the patient is given the result. In fact, the pathologist must have this degree of detachment if he or she is to function properly.

Dr Richard Asher was a distinguished London physician who had a gift for debunking enshrined medical practices, particularly its liking for cloaking ignorance in nomenclature – *'Giving something a name "fixes" something . . . words perpetuate illnesses, syndromes and signs whose existence is doubtful, they deny recognition to others whose existence is beyond question, and, moreover, they distort text book descriptions to conform to the chosen word.'*[1]

A WISH

Nor bring to watch me cease to live
Some Doctor, full of phrase and fame
To shake his sapient head and give
The ill he cannot cure – a name.

Matthew Arnold

Positive Health and the Holistic Approach
In contrast to the stress on objective diagnostic factors and the identification of disease entities, some have adopted a much more general approach. This is in line with Hans Selye's aphorism above that the emphasis should be on the person rather than the disease.

Even when a specific disease can be identified in a person, it may be impossible to predict how that person will react or whether the disease will progress. For example, some fifty years ago practically every adult in Britain will have been exposed to and harboured the tuberculosis bacillus, but only a minority will have gone on to be ill from the disease tuberculosis. It is, therefore, too simplistic to say that the tubercle bacillus is *the cause* of tuberculosis although no one becomes ill from the disease in its absence – that is, the bacillus is a necessary but not sufficient cause of tuberculosis. There are many host and environmental factors that operate to determine the clinical outcome.

1. Asher, R., *Talking Sense*. Pitman Medical, London. 1972.

It seems entirely reasonable to acknowledge that what matters in the end, is how a person feels and how his or her life progresses. In the light of this it is often pointed out that doctors and all health care workers need to adopt the holistic approach. This is in keeping with the World Health Organisation's original definition of health as being 'a state of complete, physical, mental and social well-being' (1958). This led to the fatuous objective of 'Health for all by 2000.' The downside of over-emphasising this approach is that not only may the diagnosis of particular disease be neglected, but also the individual may be denied personal responsibility for his life as the 'nanny state' takes over, intruding increasingly in all aspects of daily living. Health bureaucrats in Sweden proposed a nation-wide scheme of *'halso kontroll'*, screening the population on the justification that 'everybody is sick.'

The *Daily Telegraph* of 14th May 2009 carried a photograph of a vigorous five-year-old boy, fully airborne on his trampoline with the image of intense pleasure and joy on his face. His mother, who was a children's adviser on healthy eating, had received a warning from health officials at the Oxfordshire NHS Primary Care Trust, that her boy was 1lb over the NHS guidelines and because he was overweight he would be at risk of cancer, diabetes, heart disease and high blood pressure later in life. A spokesman for the Trust said it was following the Department of Health guidelines on the format and content of the letter. The fact that such a thing could happen shows how absurd the extremes of the 'health lobby' has become. The fact that it should be justified by officialdom makes it sinister rather than simply farcical or funny.

I have been the chairman of a Research Ethics Committee for many years. It has been depressing as well as alarming to see the army of so-called researchers and bureaucrats working on surveys and health-promoting projects that are either irrelevant or confirming the obvious. Some of these can be reduced to concepts such as the proposition that if someone is seriously ill they are not likely to be happy. This may appear to be an exaggeration, but I can assure the reader I have seen many studies at this level of uselessness.

Natural Law. Cause and Effect

Any person who expects God to 'intervene' in human affairs in general and in states of ill-health and disease, in particular, must recognise the challenge as to whether God suspends his own 'ground rules' at our behest. The great wonder of the created order is that so much of it is understandable and, to a degree, predictable, even with mankind's limited knowledge. The laws of mathematics, mechanics, physics and chemistry are understood and accepted as expressions of the ways things behave. More recent concepts of relativity have not demolished these but have added refinements and complexities that have made possible space travel and the amazing aspects of the microchip, the internet and world-wide web. These technologies have had a great spin-off in the ability to understand, investigate, diagnose and (less frequently), treat many diseases.

Historically, eminent scientists and interested observers had no difficulty in accepting these advances in knowledge and practice as activities that were God-honouring. Galileo's quarrel was never with God – quite the reverse with this reverential and devotional man. His difference was with a blinkered Catholic hierarchy. He observed plaintively, '*I do not feel obliged to believe that same God who endowed us with sense, reason, and intellect, had intended us to forgo their use.*' (*The Authority of Scripture in Philosophical Controversies*).

Nowadays, however, the wheel has gone full circle. Scientific advances prompt some to trumpet these as evidence of 'the age of man' with a corresponding exclusion of the Divine. In these times the Christian need not hesitate to point to the wonderful predictability of so many aspects of the inorganic world and much of the organic as evidences of God's work. The world is understandable, to a considerable extent, on the basis of cause and effect. Apples still do not fall upwards.

Cause and effect provide rational explanations for many aspects of human health and sickness. Recent advances, especially using the methods of epidemiology, are based on this reasoning, for example, the importance of nutrition, the effects of alcohol and tobacco, the role of activity and exercise, the contribution of genetics, the effects of radiation and so on. When I over-eat I put on weight. When I over-do it in the garden my back aches – at the very least. If I become anxious I sleep poorly. Surely, it is a matter of common sense that if there is an avoidable or remediable factor that produces undesirable symptoms, I should address the cause rather than pray about it or attend a healing service.

This also raises the question whether we should expect God to interrupt his natural order or circumvent the causal relationships between certain 'insults' and our ill-health. The Bible records God's intervention in his own physical creation when 'the winds and the waves obey him.' But the context in these examples is of a different order to that of personal healing.

Why blame God?
I have given examples where we can see cause and effect at work in the pathology of human disease and the general trend nowa-days is for an increasing proportion of human disability to be partly or wholly attributable to environmental factors. Despite this people may use examples of disease to argue against the very existence of God, and certainly of a God of goodness and benevolence.

A fascinating example of this is provided by HIV/AIDS. Prior to the recognition of this infection, the community in which it was to appear showed high prevalences of a variety of infections such as dysentery, shigellosis, herpes and venereal infections amongst male homosexuals in San Francisco. This report by Dritz and her colleagues in 1977[2] concluded by pleading for an effective

---

2. Dritz, S. K., Ainsworth, T. E., Garrard, W. F. et al., 'Patterns of sexually transmitted enteric disease in a city'. *Lancet*, 1977, 2:3-4.

vaccine. My reply to Dritz's article in the *Lancet*,[3] is probably the only time that Romans 1:27, has been quoted in the *Lancet* – and the Editor added the text as a footnote, using the Authorised Version!

The medical consequences of homosexuality are summarised, in alarming detail, as one of a series of educational pamphlets originated by the Family Research Institute Inc. (Colorado 80962, USA). This well researched and referenced pamphlet describes practices that are widespread in some homosexual communities which I cannot quote in a general work. I can only describe them as a gross abuse of the human body, as a result of which it is not in the least surprising that the result is disease.

AIDS was subsequently recognised in Los Angeles in 1981 (Center for Disease Control). The HIV virus was identified in 1983. A specific and sensitive blood test was soon available. As it became apparent that the overwhelming majority of the patients came from the male homosexual community, there was a concerted programme to minimise this fact. Full page newspaper advertisements appeared telling us 'Don't die of ignorance' or 'Anyone may catch it.' These omitted any mention of the then chief mode of transmission. They were, in fact, peddling lies. The vulnerable population were not ignorant. Nuns and celibates still do not catch it.

In due course, spread from contaminated needles and intrauterine transmission was acknowledged. There followed a general reluctance to test for the presence of the disease. In fact, clinical staff were positively dissuaded from testing for HIV. Official bodies such as The General Medical Council instructed doctors that before testing for HIV was done there should be full 'counselling.' Nothing of this nature existed for tests where there might be equally bad or worse news for the patient. There has now been a complete turn around on this policy. In some circles it appeared that the arrival of heterosexual transmission and the differing

---

3. Powell, D. E. B., 'The Gay Life'. *Lancet*, 1977, 2:140.

pattern in central and southern Africa was greeted with something approaching relief. Public health and epidemiological methods of diagnosis, screening, notification and contact tracing were never tried although they had been so successful in other infectious diseases. Professor Gordon Stewart commenting on this wrote: 'The disservice to the public, nationally and internationally, is twofold: constant exaggeration and alarm to huge majorities who are not at risk, and discounting and danger to minorities who choose or are driven to expose themselves directly and others to very high risks.'[4]

The appearance of HIV/AIDS was clearly associated with male homosexual practices in a setting where there was, and probably still is, an extraordinary degree of promiscuity, coupled with drug abuse and other practices. This was such an obvious case of cause and effect or, at least, association. Simplistic comments were made by some religious persons claiming the pandemic was God's judgement. Whilst such a view is unfortunate and cruel, especially to those who were infected gratuitously by others, during the course of medical treatment, or in utero, the fact remains that a pattern of behaviour in the great majority produced a result that was to prove so disastrous. We would do well to ponder the meaning of the warning given when Paul wrote to the Romans 2,000 years ago, that when men with men do what should be done naturally with women, they received the corresponding physical penalty in their own bodies. Recognition of the operation of cause and effect in this infection, whether homosexually or heterosexually transmitted, is neither an example of homophobia nor invoking a vindictive God.

This type of reasoning is repugnant to modern ideas amongst the establishment and politically correct. It is noticeable how often, in contemporary literature and drama, homosexuality is portrayed as misunderstood. The homosexual is usually the hero deserving of our sympathy. The AIDS patient, likewise, obtains a

4. Stewart, G. T., 'Errors in predictions of the incidence and distribution of AIDS'. *Lancet*, 1993, 1:898.

degree of priority above any other condition. The history of the acceptance and promotion of homosexuality in the twentieth century, from a public health viewpoint, has yet to be written. But the percentage of writers, producers, actors and media personalities, who have a personal commitment to homosexual life-styles and its promotion, must be well above the average. The agenda is ultimately one that is avowedly anti-God, amoral if not immoral. I see this as a contemporary example of what happened over the preceding century. Iain Murray[5] has drawn attention to the way in which fiction changed Britain through writers such as Thomas Hardy, H. G. Wells and many of their successors. Many of these people not only wrecked their own lives, but set a pattern which affected the mores of a nation.

A similar pattern has been described by Rodgers and Thompson in *Philosophers Behaving Badly*.[6] There is no hint of a Christian viewpoint in this book, but the authors present a compelling case for the argument that 'as he thinketh in his heart, so is he' (Proverbs 23:7). They describe the lives of men like Rousseau, Nietzsche, Russell, Schopenhauer, Wittgenstein, Heidegger and Foucault. These lives were disaster areas both for themselves and for those in close contact with them. In the case of Foucault they conclude he probably had HIV/AIDS and had no compunction in exposing others to the risk of being infected by him.

I have written elsewhere[7,8] making the case that HIV/AIDS should be treated on the medical model, just like any other life-threatening condition. This also applies to assessments of the prevalence of the disease and its prevention, as reported by Professor Gordon Stewart and others.[4] The strident tones adapted by the

5. Murray, I. H., *The Undercover Revolution*. Banner of Truth Trust, Edinburgh, 2009.
6. Rodgers, N and Thompson, M., *Philosophers Behaving Badly*. Peter Owen Publishers, 2005, London.
7. Powell, D. E. B., 'Morality and HIV'. MA thesis, University of Swansea, 1992.
8.——————— *AIDS and Ethics*. Ethics and Medicine, Rutherford House Medical Ethics Project, 1987, p. 34.

pro-homosexual lobby, using anti-discriminatory arguments to demand different non-medical approaches, has often had the reverse effect of impairing the proper response in the prevention and treatment of the disease. It has also promoted the spread of other diseases such as tuberculosis and malignant conditions.

The impression has been created that male homosexuality is an activity that, apart from HIV/AIDS is harmless. Whereas, in fact, it is something which carries significant medical consequences and dangers.[7] It is not a display of homophobia to point this out.

Although I have written on a variety of medical and other subjects, this is the only one in which factual comments, such as above, generated personal, hostile and even vituperative mail. This has applied to speaking at open Christian meetings. I have also received letters from distinguished epidemiologists, and several in public life who similarily have been censured for stating facts that were inconvenient to the prevailing political consensus.

4.

Age and Ageing

'There is no such thing as aging.'
Peto and Doll (1997).[1]

The distinguished epidemiologists, Sir Richard Doll and Professor Richard Peto maintained, in their 1997 contribution to the *British Medical Journal* that old age is associated with disease, but does not cause it. This was largely based on an evolutionary view. They argued that natural selection, over tens of millions of years, acted against death in early adult life rather than death in old age. Their argument was largely of a circular nature, accompanied by some fanciful mathematical models. It provided a description of old age rather than an explanation of their hypothesis.[2]

We are still left with the question whether ageing is a disease. Pathologists are generally reluctant to give 'Old Age' as a cause of death. I cannot give specific references on this topic, but I doubt whether the prevalence of death due to an unascertained cause is greater in the elderly than at younger ages. In my own experience of carrying out post-mortem examinations on elderly persons, there is almost always a detectible condition or disease present to explain the death.

Regardless of what the scientists may conjecture as to the nature of ageing we know in practice that we all get older! The rate of ageing varies widely but is inescapable. Life-expectancy has changed over man's recorded history. There have been marked swings, in both directions, over the centuries.

---

1. Peto, R., and Doll, R., 'There is no such thing as aging'. *BMJ*, 1997, 315:1030.
2. Powell, D. E. B., 'Aging has been defined as to grow or make old'. *BMJ*, 1997, 315:1531.

Increasing age is inexorably linked with the onset of the major killing diseases – cardiovascular disease, degenerative diseases (which are closely linked with the cardiovascular) and cancer. Therefore, any consideration of disease and healing is bound up with our attitude to ageing. A disease which may present as a gross aberration or intrusion in a young person may be accepted with equanimity in an aged person – at least by an observer who is significantly younger!

'Wear and tear' is a feature of all living organisms. Arterial atheroma can often be found in young people. It may not be generally appreciated that one of the biggest killers in children, apart from accident, is that of malignant disease. As we live we accumulate various 'insults' to our bodies (and possibly our minds also). This provides the basis for the advocacy of the various population screening programmes for early detection and treatment referred to above.

Ivan Illich[3] was one who gave short shrift to these aspects of the 'geriatric problem' – *'Those most hurt are certain consumers for whom the U.S. elderly can serve as a paradigm. They have been trained to experience urgent needs which no level of privilege can possibly satisfy; at the same time their ability to take care of themselves has withered, and social arrangements allowing such autonomy have practically disappeared . . . having learned to consider old age akin to disease, they developed unlimited economic needs paying for interminable therapies which are usually ineffective, frequently demeaning and painful'* . . . a sweeping statement possibly, but experience in a hospital geriatric ward or home for the elderly will substantiate its essential thrust. If it is true that the general population has, and is, being medicalised, how much more true is this in respect of the elderly.

These aspects of ageing must be important in any consideration of healing. In treatment decisions, age may be relevant to the choice of appropriate measure adopted. Thus, chemotherapy or

3. Illich, I., *Medical Nemesis.* Calder & Bryers, London, 1975.

transplantation treatments are generally much more effective in the young than in the elderly. How is this question to be understood when we look at claims of healing through faith and spiritual means? Should we then regard older people differently as far as the role of faith in their lives and illnesses? If so, what are to be our age limits for differing conditions?

Does age influence prayer for healing?

The instinctive answer to this question is surely, 'Yes.' When we are confronted by a child dying from a malignant disease, we are aghast at the tragedy. If we believe in miraculous healing in response to prayer, we will pray with unremitting intensity and encourage other like-minded believers to do the same. In contrast, when we are faced with a man in his eighties who presents with cancer in an advanced stage with metastases, we will be inclined to pray for his 'happy release.'

These contrasting attitudes reflect what we commonly see on a purely secular level amongst people who do not profess any religious belief. The agnostic materialist will be equally horrified over the plight of the dying child. Every effort will be made to eradicate that malignant disease. Radical chemotherapy and/or radiotherapy or surgery may be undertaken. In contrast, the case of the elderly man will evoke the prescription of care that concentrates on symptomatic relief to comfort and give the patient as much ease as possible – sometimes even to the point of bringing the day of death closer. Various care 'pathways' have been designed to take account of these considerations. They inevitably include age as an important factor (see below).

Should miraculous healing be ageist?

The facts discussed above add a further difficulty to the concept and practice of miraculous healing.

Why should divine intervention be limited to the younger person?

Where do we draw the line as to eligibility for miraculous healing?

How do we apply this personally?

However we may interpret the biblical references to miraculous healing, there is no hint that the age of the sufferer was considered. Practice and experience serve to highlight the contradictions in many claims for divine healing. We could even learn lessons from the secular practice of Medicine. One of the schemes which sought to deal with this problem is that of 'QUALYS' – or Quality Adjusted Life Years – although the latter is essentially a rough formula balancing cost against benefit, taking into account life-expectancy.

One of the main objections to this approach, and one which is relevant to the religious or spiritual aspect, is that generalisations do not meet individual need. No person is simply a statistic. This is at the heart of the objections to ageism. Life may be as precious to an 80-year-old man, as to a young person in 'the prime of life' – in fact, it may be even more so, in that he has that much less life expectancy left. I am sure that there are octogenarians who are enjoying a 'quality of life' far exceeding that experienced by some angst-driven, suicidal teenagers who are physically healthy.

The secular and economic attempts at 'quantifying' the quality and cost of life, have been heavily criticised by moral philosophers, purely on ethical grounds. Professor John Harris, no friend of the Christian viewpoint, criticises the QUALY approach – indeed, he goes further – *'Each person's desire to stay alive should be regarded as of the same importance and as deserving of the same respect as that of anyone else, irrespective of the quality of their life or its expected duration . . . It is sometimes said that it is a misfortune to grow old, but it is not nearly so great a misfortune as not to grow old. Growing old when you don't want to is not half the misfortune that is not growing old when you do want to.'*[4] However, Harris couples this

---

4. Harris, J., *The Value of Life*. Routledge, London, 1985, p. 101.

stress on self-awareness and autonomy, with the corollary that in their absence life ceases to be valuable – *'the value of our lives is the value we give to our lives.'*[5] This chilling attitude to the elderly infirm is a feature of the prevailing secular response to the 'problem of ageing.' Baroness Mary Warnock puts it in stark terms – *'If you're demented, you're wasting people's lives - your family's lives – and you're wasting the resources of the National Health Service.'* Warnock uses this argument in her justification of euthanasia.[6]

We need to recognise that the quality of life is changing for the elderly, at least in respect of the developed world. Samuel Johnson in his *Vanity of Human Wishes*, wrote:

> *Enlarge my life with multitude of days,*
> *In health, in sickness, thus the suppliant prays;*
> *Hides from himself his state, and shuns to know,*
> *That life protracted is protracted woe.*

In contrast, a study from Newcastle upon Tyne of 85-year-olds found that although there were significant levels of disease and impairment, these 85-year-olds had good functional ability and rated their own health as good.[7]

If secular ethicists can argue against ageism in deciding life and death issues, would it not then be perverse for the Christian who believes in, and practices prayer for miraculous healing, to confine his or her prayers to the younger age groups? The life-threatening attack of coronary thrombosis is no different in a seventy-year-old from what it is in the thirty-year-old. Surely, the practising Christian will commit himself or herself, or the loved one, to God under *all* circumstances?

5. Harris, J., in John Keown (ed.), *Euthanasia Examined,* CUP, 1995, p. 11.
6. Warnock, Mary, *Daily Telegraph*, 19th September 2008.
7. Collerton et al., 'Health and disease in 85-year-olds'. *BMJ*, 2010, 340:86.

5.

Mind and Matter

'Men ought to know that from the brain, and from the brain only, arise our pleasures, joys, laughter and jests, as well as our sorrows, pains, grief and tears. Through it in particular, we think, see, hear, distinguish the ugly from the beautiful, the bad from the good, and the pleasant from the unpleasant.'

Hippocrates (500 BC)[1]

'I will praise thee; for I am fearfully and wonderfully made: marvellous are thy works; and that my soul knoweth right well. My substance was not hid from thee, when I was made in secret, and curiously wrought in the lowest parts of the earth. Thine eyes did see my substance, yet being unperfect; and in thy book all my members were written, which in continuance were fashioned, when as yet there was none of them. How precious also are thy thoughts unto me O God! How great is the sum of them!'

Psalm 139:14-17

Any answer to questions concerning healing is conditioned by our view on the nature of man. The question 'What am I?' precedes that of 'Who am I?' The materialist will hold that all is potentially explicable on physical or material grounds – including mental states. For many, if not most, issues of life, health and disease are treated on this basis. But what if man is more than

---

1. Hippocrates, *On the Sacred Disease*, quoted in J. D. Spillane, *The Doctrine of Nerves.* Oxford University Press, 1981.

molecules? Going further, what if there are supernatural forces that are not material? Then what if there is a God, who is transcendent, and what if such a God is personal and deals with people on an individual level?

My own medical discipline and training is essentially materialistic. Part of the attraction of Pathology as a subject is that it is concerned with factors that can be observed or measured. However, regardless of what our stance is regarding matters that are of a religious or spiritual nature, there is also the realm of life which relates to the mind, thought and mental reactions. We all come to these issues from individual backgrounds which inevitably condition our attitudes. I, therefore, have to guard against being dismissive of anything that smacks of a psychological or immaterial nature. But even to someone of my own occupational viewpoint, it is obvious that the mental, immaterial realm has a major part to play in health and disease.

The person who fails to provide abnormal results to the doctor's tests, but yet obstinately persists in being ill, or even deteriorating, may constitute a reproach or even an irritation to his medical attendants. It is not unknown for patients to end up in the post-mortem room with his medical attendants stating, almost with a hint of pride, that all the tests were normal!

Sometimes the humility of the 'pure' scientist can be contrasted with that of doctors. Ideas of relativity and the quantum theory have ensured that physicists are prepared to challenge their own presuppositions, whereas doctors are often still guilty of adhering to outdated practices and assumptions. My own profession may be accused of another manifestation of this when they prefer the study of pathological processes to people. This is the equivalent of clinicians protesting that hospitals would be fine places if it were not for the patients!

There is really no excuse for this attitude on the part of doctors. After all, the basic study of Physiology along with common observation, demonstrates how the emotions can have drastic effects, not only on the functions of the body but also produce structural changes. Disorders such as hypertension, heart disturbances, peptic ulceration and changes in bowel function, and many other conditions often have a major 'mental' or psychosomatic element which triggers or perpetuates their presence. Fear, grief, anxiety may take their physical toll. When this factor can be removed or ameliorated there may be an improvement in the patient's physical problem. This is a further dimension to consider when we try to assess any claim of healing.

The pervasiveness of fear

Can there be such a thing as a completely fearless person? Lord Moran's book *The Anatomy of Courage*[2] was dedicated to *'my father who was without* fear, *by his son who is less fortunate'* – a filial phrase, but an impossible claim. Fear can take so many forms. Whilst we may 'dread the blows we never feel', we may also succumb to that which we fear with a frequency that often appears to be more than coincidental. No surgeon welcomes the patient who resists surgery with the threat 'I'll not recover – I will die', because all too often he may do so.

Even a disease as 'organic' as cancer may be affected by emotional factors. Cases have been reported of patients with disseminated cancer becoming extremely depressed – even when allowance is made for their dire state. Suicide may be attempted. In some cases when the depression was treated with electroconvulsive therapy, not only did the depression disappear, but so did the tumours. Dr Brad Burke gives many references to the reported instances of the effects, both beneficial and harmful, of emotional states on disease.[3] It is important to note that Burke underlines that it is not only Christian faith that may have health benefits, but that *any* faith will do. This may apply to adverse effects also! Burke's contribution illustrates the need for caution in interpreting cause and effect when we analyse claims for cure in many diseases.

2. Moran, Lord, *The Anatomy of Courage.* Constable, London, 1945.
3. Burke, B., *Does God Still Do Miracles?* Victor. Kingsway Communications, Eastbourne, 2006, p. 55.

Perhaps W. H. Auden was on to something when he wrote on the death of Miss Edith Gee –

> '*Dr Thomas sat over his dinner,*
> *Though his wife was waiting to ring,*
> *Rolling his bread into pellets*
> *Said 'Cancer's a funny thing'.*
> *Nobody knows what the cause is,*
> *Though some pretend they do.*
> *It's like some hidden assassin*
> *Waiting to strike at you.*
> *Childless women get it,*
> *And men when they retire;*
> *It's as if there had to be some outlet*
> *For their failed creative fire.'*

Suffering conveys fear to those not directly involved – thus contact with cancer reminds us of our own mortality; contact with the bereaved may make us fear for our own loved ones just as witnessing suffering which we can do little or nothing to alleviate may be the most intense of all forms of affliction.

The above raises the question of mental illness in its more extreme forms. I have little experience or expertise in psychiatry and, therefore, restrict my comments to that which is observable and relevant to the main question. But there is no doubt that psychotic disorders, such as schizophrenia and bipolar disorder, carry with them significant morbidity as far as physical problems are concerned. An added difficulty is that these associated conditions are difficult to disentangle from the side effects of anti-psychotic drugs. They also raise the question of the distinction between mental illness and the concept of mental disturbance that Christians might see as spiritual problems. I shall return to this later.

In my medical student days, the study of psychiatry under eminent psychiatrists such as Sir David Henderson, appeared straightforward. Everyone could be classified as sane or insane. The sane could be further subdivided in the psychoneurotics and the remainder. Now, however, shades of grey dominate. The depressive may have a schizoid personality which avoids labelling him as either neurotic or schizophrenic.

Difficulties in Definition and Diagnosis

The experiences of daily life with its stresses and strains affect all of us in some way or another. The ways in which we react or cope vary considerably, both in respect of mental and physical responses.

This applies to severe mental disturbances. Thomas Szasz can write a book on *The Myth of Mental Illness*.[4] Other psychiatrists may attach the latest label of mental disorder without any hesitation – *'Psychiatrists do not diagnose their patients like other doctors do. They discard four of their senses and literally play it by ear . . . presenting symptoms are elevated to the status of a disease like varieties of fever were in the eighteenth century. The pharmaceutical industry provides corresponding antidotes and reinforces the illusion.'* In this field, as in so many others, it is a matter of balance. Dr Alexander Comfort is in no doubt that he *'would rather see a relative of mine treated by a psychiatrist who had read both about Szasz and about serotonin, than by one who, through his own personal difficulties, refused to entertain one or other of these.'*

A woman of 57 developed rheumatoid arthritis for which cortisone was prescribed. She had been a happy, home-loving person but quite suddenly became miserable and complained of severe abdominal and chest pain. Her own doctor could not find any evidence of disease, and in view of the discrepancy between her anguished complaints and the absence of signs, he called in a psychiatrist. Following a rough ambulance ride to the neighbouring mental hospital, she was admitted on the

---

4. Szasz, T. S., *The Myth of Mental Illness*. Harper & Row, London, 1945.

third day of her illness and died there two days later. The husband and family protested throughout that she was seriously ill. Post-mortem examination revealed cortisone-induced ulceration of the stomach which had perforated, giving rise to peritonitis and empyema. The final irony was that the deceased had a 'phobia' of taking cortisone because a relative had died from its side-effects.

What about the eccentric?

In an increasingly conformist society, where 'Big Brother' has eyes in unexpected places, eccentrics are at a premium. When they do emerge they are often perceived as an irritant to the more conventional. If the problem of defining normality is a problem in physical disease, it is probably even greater in the case of mental disorder.

It was a quiet, but stiflingly hot, summer afternoon, when I was on duty in the sick-bay of my shore base, doing my National Service in the Royal Navy. My reveries were suddenly shattered when the Master at Arms, accompanied with other naval ratings, burst into the Sick Bay, shouting 'Doc! Doc!' Between them they were gripping violently a red-faced Able Seaman. It transpired that this young rating had been on duty in the Armoury, when he took it into his head to leave with a loaded pistol; proceed to the ratings mess, where, without any preamble or word, he carefully took successive shots at the hanging light bulbs, finally silencing the Mess radio (or wireless as it was at that time) – all of which he hit with unerring accuracy.

When I attended to the sailor, he was quiet and frightened. I admitted him to one of the beds in the Sick Bay. In no time, the Station Commander was on the phone to me, more or less ordering me to certify him as 'mad' and get him transported

5. Scull, A., *Hysteria: The Biography*. Oxford University Press, 2009.

under arrest to Detention Quarters. I played for time and eventually obtained agreement for the man's referral to the Naval Psychiatrist at the RN Hospital at Haslar. I do not know the eventual outcome, but in the short term, the man was returned to normal duty. The psychiatrist and I agreed that the man might be an asset in conditions of armed conflict!

Hysteria

Andrew Scull has written a book *Hysteria: The Biography*.[5] In this he charts and describes the infinite variety of symptoms that may be packaged with the diagnosis of hysteria. The idea is that an ailment may itself have a lifespan. The presentation may vary with the passage of time and in different social settings. The symptoms range over choking sensations, paralysis, pain anywhere, hypochondria, fatigue, voicelesness and many others. The postulated causes have been as various as a wandering womb, brain conditions, neurological disease, focal sepsis, etc. The treatments have been correspondingly numerous and bizarre, including purging, bleeding, uterine fixation, removal of the clitoris, hysterectomy and ovariotomies (at a time when a third of the patients died), and electric shocks applied to the brain, tongues or genitals. Sigmund Freud claimed that sexual repression was the cause of all hysteria.[6]

I refer to this subject because it is a good illustration of the scope for mistaken diagnosis and for claims of cure for conditions that are incapable of scientific or rational analysis. Christians are by no means immune from these manifestations. Some may even be more susceptible to them.

This line of thought, however, can easily go in another direction, as a result of over-stressing the importance of mind over matter. This may infect some religious attitudes and practices.

---

6. Moore, W., 'The Life Stories of Diseases' (review of above). *BMJ*, 2009, 339:1034.

Positive Thinking

Norman Vincent Peale, in his book *The Power of Positive Thinking*, popularised the notion that many of life's problems can be overcome as a result of our attitudes to them. This has spilled over into the area of health and disease. It has also infiltrated religious responses to them. Who would argue against approaches that through methods of relaxation, psychotherapy, or whatever, induce a happier state of mind? However, it is a different matter when this approach is based on the claim that the altered state of mind or positive attitude acts, for example, through the immune system to counter the disease. Positive thinking then becomes a method of treatment. Furthermore, if the disease does not respond the blame lies with the patient's inability or unwillingness to embark on this method. Polly Toynbee[7] quotes Martin Seligman, a former president of the American Psychological Association, as claiming that 'happy people have feistier immune systems than less happy people.' Toynbee fairly concludes: 'The invasion of unscientific positivism into the field of psychology is alarming.' I would add, so it is for Christianity (see below).

This approach has been prominent amongst Christian Science followers and other sects. I think it is undeniable that an element of this type of thinking has been taken up in some charismatic circles when believers have been encouraged to think that wealth, happiness and health are all part of the package received 'by faith.'

All this is part of mankind's search for happiness. It is then small wonder that some unexpected bedfellows are found making common cause of this theme. The Dalai Lama has adapted Buddhism to the way to happiness. Others such as Abbot Christopher Jamison claim the monastic life can be a way of fulfilment.

Barbara Ehrenreich has written a book *Smile or Die*.[8] She contracted breast cancer and experienced the pressure to be

---

7. Toynbee, P., 'Always look on the bright side of life?', *BMJ*, 2009, 339:b5494.
8. Ehrenreich, B., *Smile or Die: How Positive Thinking Fooled America and the World.* Granta Books, 2009.

'positive' as part of the 'pink ribbon' scene. She exposes the American 'have a nice day' culture and the way in which it encourages false optimism – not only in the field of health, but generally in the world of business. She even argues that *'Positive thinking destroyed the economy,'* because of the state of mind of people like Dick Fuld of the ill-fated bank, Lehmann Brothers. Julian Baggini in commenting on this book (*Daily Telegraph*, 13th January 2010) said that what worried him was that *'our pursuit of happiness is leading us to judge the great intellectual and spiritual traditions of the past according to one only measure: do they increase happiness and reduce misery? . . . The result is that wisdom is hollowed out and replaced with a soft centre of caramelised contentment.'* So it is that we have 'mindfulness' classes at famous public schools and a Mindfulness Centre with a professor at Oxford. Baggini concludes: *'We are witnessing deep thought being driven out by positive thought.'*

I believe that all this should encourage the Christian to think and not resort to glib formulae. It is regrettable that sometimes we see atheists and agnostics showing a rationality that is an object lesson to some of the woolly claims made by a variety of religious adherents – including some of a Christian persuasion.

6.

Is Materialism Enough?

'The baby new to earth and sky,
What time his tender palm is prest
Against the circle of the breast,
Has never thought that "this is I".

But as he grows he gathers much,
And learns the use of 'I' and 'me',
And finds "I am not what I see
And other than the things I touch".'

Tennyson,
'In Memoriam', XLV

'There are more things in heaven and earth, Horatio,
Than are dreamt of in your philosophy.'

Shakespeare, 'Hamlet'

Any person reading this will be in one of two major groups. He or she may belong to those who are thorough-going materialists. Such believe that all human beings are ultimately animals whose structure, personality and behaviour can be reduced to constituents of chemistry, physics and physiology. On this basis all human behaviour can be explained in terms of what is material. If there are functions or emotions that are not readily understood this simply reflects our ignorance. It is unfair to criticise people of this viewpoint on the basis that they deny the reality of beauty, truth, love and all that goes to enhance human life. They simply rest their case in ignorance that may be enlightened as human life continues to evolve and explain what has not been understood.

The other person is one who does not accept this strict biological view of human life. Such a man or woman believes that there is more to life – in fact, much more. These people believe there is some entity which cannot be measured or seen. There is 'something else' that goes to constitute the essential person. This may be called a soul or spirit or many other names. The materialistic viewpoint is so ingrained (at least in Western society) that even consideration of the soul, or its equivalent, may invite a materialistic analysis. Fenwick and Fenwick in their book, *The Art of Dying*,[1] refer to attempts made to measure a loss of weight at the point of death as the soul leaves the body or changes in the surrounding electromagnetic energy!

Any attempt to 'prove' the existence of the human soul is akin to these crude attempts to define it in terms of the material. It is striking that from early history, all societies have shown evidence of an intuitive belief that human life is more than simple animal existence, and that it is preserved in some form after death. Belief in the transcendent is a characteristic of being a human person. The uniqueness of each individual is part of this.

The differences between these two approaches are profound and inherently irreconcilable. The belief in the view that each person is an eternal soul is at the heart of any consideration of questions of disease and healing, whether natural or spiritual. Ultimately, this has to be a matter of faith. I would, nevertheless, maintain that this faith does not have to, or should, be one that flies in the face of facts or become the shelter for wish-fulfilment. We also have to accept that, at least in Western Society, the overwhelming viewpoint as to the nature of man is materialistic. D. M. Amstrong expresses it: *'I conclude that it is the scientific vision of man, and not the philosophical or religious or artistic or*

1. Fenwick, P. and Fenwick, E., *The Art of Dying, A Journey to Elsewhere.* Continuum, London, 2008.

moral vision of man, that is the best clue we have to the nature of man. And it is rational to argue from the best evidence we have.'[2]

In the early days of the movement towards the legalisation of abortion, we used to hear references to 'the sanctity of life.' This phrase is now seldom heard, or if it is, it has a quaintness which often invokes impatient dismissal. Over thirty years ago people like Francis Schaeffer[3] pleaded for recognition of the divide that was being crossed. Is human life unique? Is there really any difference between human and animal life?

Prominent philosophers have given eloquent expression to sentiments that would have left a previous generation aghast. Peter Singer wrote:[4] *'Whatever the future holds, it is likely to prove impossible to restore in full the sanctity-of-life view . . . We can no longer base our ethics on the idea that human beings are a special form of creation, made in the image of God, singled out from all other animals, and alone possessing an immortal soul.'* The inevitable result of this reasoning is the conclusion that a human is not necessarily of greater worth than an animal. *'If we compare a severely defective human infant with a non-human animal, a dog or a pig, for example, we will often find the nonhuman to have superior capacities. . .'*

Professor John Harris is another who has written at length on this topic,[5] but is prepared, at least explicitly, to go further than Singer, as his logic leads him. Harris asks *'What makes human life valuable?'* He divides human beings into 'persons' and 'non-persons' and therefore value does not accrue by virtue of being human. Non-persons have no right to have their life protected. Newborn babes cannot be regarded as persons. 'It is the *capacity* to value one's own life that is crucial' and he stresses the importance of

2. Armstrong, D. M., 'The Nature of the Mind', in *The Mind-Brain Identity Theory*, ed. C. V. Borst. MacMillan, London, 1970, p. 68.
3. Schaeffer, F., *The Great Evangelical Disaster*. Kingsway Publications Ltd., Eastbourne, 1984, p. 103.
4. Singer, P., 'Sanctity of Life or Quality of Life'. *Pediatrics*, 1983, 128.
5. Harris, J., *The Value of Life*. Routledge, London, 1985.

awareness and self-consciousness. Harris has no problem with the practice of suicide, assisted suicide or voluntary euthanasia. In fact, '*to frustrate the wish to die will on this view be as bad as frustrating the wish to live, for in each case we would be negating the value that the individuals themselves put on their lives.*'

Professor L. Wolpert gave the Lloyd-Roberts lecture to the London Royal College of Physicians in 1986, on the subject 'Science and anti-science.'[6] Wolpert writes as a humanist, rationalist and atheist. He begins by pointing out the existence of a critical and deep-seated fear of scientific inquiry. At the same time belief in the paranormal, astrology and fringe medicine are on the increase. It is claimed that two-thirds of people read their horoscope and 75% believe astrology to be scientific. Wolpert emphasises the distinction between science and technology because science involves modes of thought which may be psychologically uncomfortable. Thus, science has been attacked by sociologists and philosophers under the guise of relativism – all beliefs become valid and 'Scientific truth is an illusion'. Another of Wolpert's comments relevant to our subject is his claim that there is a strong similarity between this type of thinking with that of those who accept the paranormal and support holistic medicine. A result of this is that disproof of such ideas (and, I would add the denial of the miraculous) becomes impossible. I would maintain that the stance of people like Wolpert can be 'good' for professing Christians. The danger is that Christians may avoid thinking when they move in their own circles. There are times and issues when we are meant to 'contend' for the faith, rather than engage in automatic denial.

This is where people like Wolpert may find support from the most unlikely of people. Jonathan Edwards (1703-1758) had no time for Christians who were not prepared to think and discern. Such people '. . . *looked upon critical inquiries into the difference between true grace and its counterfeits, or at least being very busy in*

6. Walpert, L., 'Science and anti-science'. *J. Roy. Coll. Phys.*, London, 1987, 21:159.

such enquiries and spending time in them, to be impertinent and unreasonable; tending rather to damp the work of the Spirit of God rather than promote it . . . The cry was, "Oh, there is no danger if we are but lively in religion and full of God's Spirit and live by faith, of being misled!"' One of Edwards's major themes was the danger of the outward manifestations of, what he called *'the religious affections'*, being a distraction, or even a deceit, from that of true religion.[7]

The role of faith in any assessment of the nature of human life is bound up with our attitude to that of the origin of man, the creation and the acknowledgement of God and his primary work in all these. The alternative has to be a world of accident and ultimate meaninglessness. It then becomes fatuous even to consider the possibility of healing by any agency other than that of the biological. After all, this must, by definition, be beyond the bounds of possibility. There remain more than enough difficulties, in confronting the question, for those who accept the basis that we live in a created world that has meaning and that we as human beings are part of God's creation and that our essential beings, or souls, have an eternal destiny.

Pain and Personality
Whether we are religious, agnostic or completely atheistic, we should, I believe, do well to acknowledge the mystery which constitutes so much of human life. Professor Raymond Tallis has published an extraordinary book entitled *The Kingdom of Infinite Space – a fantastical journey around your head.*[8] He candidly declares his position in his introduction that: *'I do not believe that we are immortal souls, unhappy lodgers trapped in 70 kilograms of protoplasm.'* He goes on to *'equally reject the notion that we are entirely identified with our bodies.'* Whilst Tallis disavows any religious belief he exposes the utter inadequacy of a purely scientific

---

7. Edwards, Jonathan, *The Religious Affections.* Select Works, Vol. 3. Banner of Truth Trust, Edinburgh, 1961.
8. Tallis, R., *The Kingdom of Infinite Space.* Atlantic Books, London, 2008.

approach. Although he leaves the main question unanswered, he faces and exposes the inadequacy of materialism with stark honesty – *'Selves are not cooked up, or stored, in brains or (as writers such as the late Francis Crick would have it) in bits of brain, such as the claustrum. Selves require bodies as well as brains, material environments as well as bodies, and societies as well as material environments. That is why, despite the hype, we won't find in the brain an explanation of ourselves, or the secret of a better self or happier life . . . consciousness is not to be found in the brain.'*

Tallis goes on to expand his consideration of the human person in dealing with pain and suffering. *'Suffering seems to be halfway between being and having; we say, "I have toothache", but after a while we might just as well say "I am toothache" or "Toothache has me" . . . At first suffering seems to be an interruption coming between me and myself. I go to sleep and hope it will pass away and I will no longer have to live it out. Sooner or later, if it persists, it will no longer be outside of me: it will be me as outside.'* Pain and suffering take over. In this way we can distinguish between *feeling* hunger, from the more intense 'I *am* hungry.'

Tallis applies the same argument to feelings of pleasure and delight, but then *'We fear our carnal luck will not hold out. We are right.'*

These considerations provide a corrective to mere mechanistic considerations of pain. No one has written (or put into practice) more convincingly, on the usefulness and need for pain than the distinguished surgeon, the late Paul Brand. He wrote, with Philip Yancey, of *'Pain: the Gift Nobody Wants'*.[9] Brand's main insight is into the way in which the sensations of touch, pain, heat and cold are essential for health or even life itself. Sensibility is a 'gift' that ensures our survival. However, Brand also recognises the psychological factors that may intensify pain far beyond any utility that might be of benefit. He pulls no punches, for example, in admitting the dangers of 'medicalisation', when he states: *'The*

9. Brand, P. and Yancey, P., *Pain: The Gift Nobody Wants.* Marshall Pickering & Harper Collins, London, 1993.

word hospital comes from the Latin for "guest", but in some modern hospitals "victim" seems more apt.' He quotes Oliver Sacks:

> 'One's own clothes are replaced by an anonymous white nightgown, one's wrist is clasped by an identification bracelet with a number. One becomes subject to institutional rules and regulations. One is no longer a free agent; one no longer has rights; one is no longer in the "world-at-large". It is strictly analogous to becoming a prisoner, and humiliatingly reminiscent of one's first day at school. One is no longer a person – one is now an inmate.'
>
> (Oliver Sachs, *A Leg to Stand On*, 1984).

> *'A mother of three children was left paralysed after sneezing. She was found to have ruptured a disc in her spine. She had to be spoon-fed her meals. The associated pain became so intense that she said later that 'I eventually got to the point where I just didn't want to live. The pain completely took over every part of my life'. She became suicidal. Surgery, involving the insertion of a metal cage, bolts and a spring device, brought relief and cure.'*
>
> (*Daily Telegraph*, 29th October 2009).

This type of case illustrates the way in which pain becomes the issue, but also supports Brand's emphasis on the way in which it may direct attention to its cause. The greater difficulty is when pain is intense, irremediable and even 'purposeless' in that it does not lead to the unmasking of some silent primary cause. This can be true in many painful conditions, such as chronic back pain, post-herpetic neuralgia, migraine, trigeminal neuralgia and many other non-specific conditions.

The complexity of attempts to define human personality and its origin in purely physical or chemical terms is well seen in some cases of the 'Locked-in Syndrome'. This is graphically illustrated by Jean-Dominique Bauby. Bauby had a sudden stroke which left him speechless and paralysed. He initially appeared to be in a state of oblivion and would have remained as such if the fact that he could blink an eyelid had not been noticed by the surgeon who was on the point of suturing the lids together. There followed the incredible account of how he communicated with his speech therapist, Sandrine, so that he was able to write the moving account of his illness, by simply blinking his eyelid (*The Diving Bell and the Butterfly*, Fourth Estate, 1997). Bauby died in 1997 – not when he appeared to do so at the time of his stroke, but when all signs of death occurred at which time his personality no longer existed in human form.

Another example of the 'locked-in syndrome' is the reported case of Tony Nicklinson (*Daily Telegraph*, 20th July 2010). Mr Nicklinson, age 56, a former engineer and rugby fanatic, suffered a major stroke which left him totally dependant. He could communicate only by blinking and nodding at letters on a board. By these means he described his plight – '*I cannot scratch if I itch. I cannot pick my nose if it is blocked and I can only eat if I am fed like a baby – only I won't grow out of it like a baby. I have no privacy or dignity left. I am washed, dressed and put to bed by carers who are, after all, still strangers.*' Sadly, the purpose of his communication was to plead for release by means of assisted suicide. Regardless of how views as to the management of such patients may vary widely, both underline the divorce between gross cerebral and neurological malfunction with near perfect preservation of personality.

Much of the above may well appear to confuse the main issue with respect as to whether healing may occur miraculously or in some way which is completely inexplicable on natural grounds. All I would plead for is a degree of reticence when we are confronted by events that are 'beyond our ken.' This is especially the case when we see the way in which atheists and agnostics acknowledge that the nature of personhood is in the ultimate analysis not known or understood. It should also ensure that the religious devotee should think before jumping to the conclusion that his or her God has intervened miraculously!

Attitudes and Acupuncture

Attempts are and have been made to justify the claimed efficacy of acupuncture in the relief of pain, based on physiological mechanisms. I have yet to see a coherent hypothesis that might explain in any detail how the insertion of needles at preselected points based on meridians or whatever has a rational basis. The first question is still whether acupuncture works and in what conditions.

Drs Cappernauld, Cooper and Saltoun visited China in March 1972 and published a report in the *Lancet*.[10] They witnessed a wide variety of major surgical operations and dental extractions. They saw patients speak to their surgeons during the course of an operation and even eat small slices of apple or orange. They then add the vague, unspecified comment that the main advantage of acupuncture anaesthesia was in the *reduction of dosage* (my italics) of conventional therapy applied in the form of coeliac-plexus blocks, local anaesthesia, barbiturate premedication and intravenous pethidine and promethazine during the course of the operation. These last comments, in my opinion, completely negate their preceding claims.

Another anecdotal account was published by Dr P. E. Brown, a general practitioner who toured Chinese hospitals in March and April 1972.[11] There are numerous reports of this nature. If there is a general effect, the question remains regardless of any scientific neuro-physiological explanation, whether there is something happening other than that of the well known placebo phenomenon.

In 1984, Dr Petr Skrabanek[12] could barely contain his exasperation with the continuing claims of efficacy, not only for the anaesthetic but also dramatic healing effects of acupuncture. He wrote: 'In

---

10. Cappernauld, I., Cooper, E., Saltoun, D., 'Acupuncture in China'. *Lancet*, 1972, 2:1136.
11. Brown, P. E., 'Use of Acupuncture in Major Surgery'. *Lancet*, 1972, 1:1328.
12. Skrabanek, P., 'Acupuncture and the Age of Unreason'. *Lancet*, 1984, 1:1169.

my opinion, what is at issue is the complex problem of demarcation between science and quackery, between reason and faith, between honest search for truth and unscrupulous exploitation of human suffering.' He adds a comment that is relevant to the purpose of this book. He criticises an editorial in the *British Medical Journal* which argued that if acupuncture provides effective and safe pain relief then its mechanism is of secondary importance – 'Perhaps the less it is investigated, the better for its effectiveness; this would certainly be true of miracle cures.' Although Skrabanek writes from a humanist, godless stance, I find his plain speaking and rationalism in this type of argument irresistible. The Christian should not need to resort to obscurantism to substantiate his faith in an almighty God.

Skrabanek, and others, responded in similar fashion when the *Lancet* published the first randomised, double-blind trial of homeopathic medicine with placebo.[13] One contributor described this as 'the tail of absurdity wagging the sick dog of rationality.' Another wrote: 'If a "non-drug" is effective, a new physics and a new chemistry will have been born.' Skrabanek tore into the attack with a devastating analysis: 'Homeopathy is a belief system with its prophet (Hahnemann), sacred test (*Organon*), rituals (proving, succession, trituration), and logic . . . The critique of homoeopathy by Sir James Young Simpson and the rebuttal of homoeopathy by Oliver Wendell Holmes should be read by all those who are attracted by the light of homoeopathy.' I quote these comments mindful of the fact that some prominent evangelicals, noted for the rigour of their rationality, such as the late Dr Martyn Lloyd Jones have been sympathetic to practitioners of homoeopathy. All of which may serve to underline the impossibility of complete consistency in our thinking as we approach the issues relating to health and disease – not to mention our interpretation of the Bible and claims of healing.

---

13. Skrabanek, P., 'Is Homeopathy a Placebo Response?', *Lancet*, 1986, 2:1107.
O'Keefe, D., p. 1106.
Khan, M. F., p. 1107.

Religion as a placebo

Just as Skrabanek, above, recognised that procedures such as acupuncture may have beneficial effects, so it is possible that religion may work at this level – and it may be that any old religion will do!

Drs Galanter and Diamond of the Albert Einstein College of Medicine, New York, described a collaborative group study of two sects over a period of 7 years.[14] These were the Divine Light Mission (followers of the Guru Maharaj Ji) and The Unification Church (followers of Sun Myung Moon). I note that the authors have their own eccentric conception of what constitutes an 'evangelical!' Many of the members of the sects had had a high incidence of pre-existing drug dependency before joining. They observed a marked change in these addictions and a reduction in neurotic symptom scores. Their conclusions were that '. . . it is probable that joining a religious group was effective in providing relief because it was introduced to the individual at a time when change was sought and it provided a new social structure within which activities could gain a new meaning. Thus, as shown by these studies, the stronger the commitment to the group the better one feels.' Can orthodox Christian claims always be distinguished from such examples? When professing Christians congregate in large numbers and set out to create a highly emotional atmosphere in which persons, particularly young ones suffering from psychological disabilities, are pressurised to 'yield' or confess, is this essentially different from what some of these sects practice?

14. Galanter, M. and Diamond, L. C., 'Relief of Psychiatric Symptoms in evangelical sects'. *Brit. J. Hosp. Med.*, 1981, p. 495.

7.

The Biblical Record of Healing

'I am the Lord that healeth thee' (Exodus 15:26).

The Old Testament has many accounts of various diseases. It records instances of resurrection or resuscitation. There are only three instances of healing of the body apart from the countless ones healed by looking at the brazen serpent (see below). For this reason, and for the sake of concentration, I largely confine consideration to what the New Testament has to say. This entails the accounts we have from the life of Jesus and the witness of the early Christian Church.

HEALING IN THE NEW TESTAMENT

Matthew

4:23   Jesus healing every disease . . .
8:2   Jesus healing the man with leprosy.
8:5   Jesus healing the centurion's servant.
8:14   Jesus healing Peter's mother-in-law of a fever.
8:28   Jesus healing two demon-possessed men.
9:2   Jesus healing the paralytic.
9:18   Jesus raising the ruler's dead daughter
9:20   Jesus healing the woman with bleeding.
9:27   Jesus healing two blind men.
9:32   Jesus healing the man demon-possessed and dumb.

9:35   Jesus healing every disease and sickness.
10:1   Jesus giving power to his disciples to heal every disease
        and sickness.
10:8   Jesus giving power to his disciples to raise the dead.
11:4   Jesus claims healing of blind, lame, leprosy, deaf and
        dead.
11:21, 23 A blitz of miracles.
12:22   Jesus heals the man demon-possessed, blind and dumb.
15:22   Jesus heals the demon-possessed daughter.
15:30   Jesus heals the lame, blind, crippled, dumb, and many
        others.
17:14   Jesus heals the son suffering from seizures.
20:30   Jesus heals two blind men.
21:14   Jesus heals the blind and lame.
27:52   Many buried raised to life.

Mark

1:25   Jesus heals the man possessed by an evil spirit.
1:30   Jesus heals Simon's mother-in-law from a fever.
1:32   Jesus heals all the sick and demon-possessed.
1:34   Jesus heals many of various diseases.
1:40   Jesus heals the man with leprosy.
2:3   Jesus heals the paralysed man.
3:1   Jesus heals the man with a shrivelled hand.
3:10   Jesus heals many.
5:2   Jesus heals the man with an evil spirit.
5:22   Jesus raises Jairus's daughter.
5:25   Jesus heals the woman who was bleeding.
6:55   Jesus heals all who came to him.
7:25   Jesus heals the daughter possessed by an evil spirit.
7:32   Jesus heals the man who was deaf and dumb.
8:23   Jesus heals the blind man at the pool of Bethsaida.
9:17   Jesus heals the son with seizures – whom the disciples
        had failed to heal.

10:46   Jesus heals blind Bartimaeus.
16:17-20   Jesus promises miraculous power to his disciples.

Luke

4:27   Jesus affirms the healing of leprosy in the case of Naaman.
4:33   Jesus heals the man possessed by a demon.
4:38   Jesus heals Simon's mother-in-law from a fever.
4:40   Jesus heals all with various kinds of sickness
5:12   Jesus heals the man with leprosy.
5:15   Jesus heals many of their sicknesses.
6:6   Jesus heals the man with a shrivelled hand.
6:18   Jesus heals many of their diseases.
7:2   Jesus heals the centurion's son.
7:12   Jesus raises the son of the widow of Nain.
7:21   Jesus heals many of various diseases.
8:2   Jesus heals Mary Magdalene of seven demons.
8:27   Jesus heals a demon-possessed man.
8:41   Jesus raises Jairus's daughter.
8:43   Jesus heals the woman who was bleeding.
9:38   Jesus heals the son who had seizures.
13:11   Jesus heals the crippled woman.
17:12   Jesus heals ten men who had leprosy.
18:35   Jesus heals the blind beggar.
22:51   Jesus heals the servant's ear.

John

4:46   Jesus heals the official's son.
5:5   Jesus heals an invalid at the pool of Bethesda.
6:2   Jesus heals the sick.
9:1   Jesus heals the man blind from birth.
11:1   Jesus raises Lazarus from the tomb.

HEALINGS IN THE EARLY CHRISTIAN CHURCH

Acts

3:2 Peter and John heal the cripple at the Beautiful Gate of the temple.

5:15 The apostles healed many and all who came.

9:17 Ananias restores Paul's sight.

9:36 Peter raises Dorcas.

14:8 Paul heals the crippled man at Lystra.

19:12 Paul heals by indirect contact.

20:9 Paul restores Eutychus following his fall.

28:3 Paul survives the venomous snake-bite.

28:8 Paul heals Publius's father from fever and dysentery.

28:9 Paul heals the sick islanders.

The Epistles

1 Corinthians 12:9 . . . to another gifts of healing.

James 5:14 . . . anointing for the sick.

3 John 2 . . . John's prayer that Gaius should be in good health.

It can be seen that there is a striking pattern in the accounts found in the Bible. Miraculous healing is seldom mentioned in the Old Testament, although God's miraculous intervention in the lives of individuals and the nations is a recurring theme. The God who is described is none other than the God of creation who is almighty as well as intimately involved in the world and life which he had brought into being. Despite this, the instances of God intervening directly in human disease are few.

Sarah and Abraham were infertile until they were in their nineties and had even tried surrogacy before Sarah conceived. Elijah raised the widow of Zarephath's son (1 Kings 17:17-24). Elisha was instrumental in the healing of Namaan's leprosy

(2 Kings 5:10-19). Then there is the strange case of an unidentified man, who revived during his burial when he touched the bones of Elisha in the sepulchre (2 Kings 13:20, 21).

The example of Job is a case of its own. Job could be used to back many arguments, including some which would appear to be mutually contradictory – such as, God's role in the infliction or allowing of disease and his part in coping with suffering as well as healing from it. Much of the book is devoted to God's *non*-intervention.

The psalmists certainly sing of physical and mental suffering – for example, in Psalms 22, 32, 38, 39, 69 and 102. However, I fail to see how any of these provide the basis for a coherent case or description of the causes of disease, or their cure, whether by natural or supernatural means.

Taking the Old Testament as a whole, we are given a picture of the God who is almighty, eternal and intimately involved in the affairs of men, on a grand scale. But, apart from these, almost unique, exceptions, human life in the centuries covered by the writings, continued on its course of birth, life and death amongst God's people and the pagan world, in their uninterrupted courses. Whatever doctrine we may deduce from the Old Testament, one of miraculous faith healing for our day does not appear to be justified.

The New Testament

In the New Testament the incidents are overwhelmingly those of miracles worked by Jesus himself. Furthermore, even these are largely localised to the early part of his public ministry. If the accounts were plotted graphically against time a marked clustering would be evident. John's gospel has the centrepiece of Lazarus's resurrection, but only four other instances. The Acts again has a cluster of miracles. The Epistles however, do not give any accounts, but simply give two specific references to the gift of healing.

I am aware that the way in which I have presented the above may well read as taking a negative or critical stance. However, it is surely vital that we base our attitude on both the Bible and the evidence of experience and history. I also accept that the truth, or even the importance, of any doctrine does not depend on the frequency with which we find it in Scripture. Furthermore, there are clear references which would appear to support the exercise of supernatural or miraculous healing in the Christian church. Jesus **did** give power to his 12 disciples to 'heal all manner of sickness and all manner of disease' (Matthew 10:1); he did tell them to 'heal the sick, cleanse the lepers, raise the dead, cast out devils' (Matthew 10:8) and the gift of healings is included amongst those given to the early Christian church (1 Corinthians 12:9).

The New Testament miracles of healing are broadly of two classes. First, there are the miracles which were an expression of God's compassion and are usually linked with the exercise of faith on the part of the recipient or his or her attendants. For example, Matthew chapter 9 emphasises both the faith of the woman suffering from menorrhagia, the blind men and Jairus, as well as the compassion which moved Jesus as he saw the crowds.

The second group are those miracles that signified God's presence and power. In the third chapter of Acts we have the story of the man who was born lame. He begged money from Peter and John. They had none to give him, but instead healed him in the name of Jesus Christ. There is no hint of faith on the part of the lame man. But he proved to be a test case at the inception of the New Testament Church. His presence discomfited Christ's enemies as well as authenticating Christ's apostles. Many turned to Christ as a result. When the apostles were arraigned before the Jewish ecclesiastical rulers, this unnamed man became the touchstone of Christ's continuance and the fact that the apostles were his representatives – *'And now, Lord, behold their threatenings: and grant unto thy servants, that with all boldness they may speak thy word, by stretching forth thine hand to heal; and that signs and wonders may be done by the name of thy holy child Jesus.'* (Acts 4:29, 30).

If we do not accept the Bible as authoritative, there is no problem. Some may regard any, or all, of the above as inaccurate, untrue or mythical. If, however, we accept the Bible as the word of God, this will determine our attitude to the question of miraculous healing in our time. But even amongst believers our responses may vary –

1. We may accept that God can, has and does intervene to heal miraculously in response to human prayer and faith. We may go further and believe that God does this regularly and that it is even part of the salvation that comes to the believer as the result of Christ's death and atonement.

2. Whilst we accept the biblical record, we may believe that such miracles ceased during succeeding years. Thus, Bishop J. C. Ryle had no problem. When commenting on the portion in Mark 16: 17 and 18, where Jesus told the disciples that they would place their hands on the sick and they would recover, he commented (leaving aside any question as to the canonicity of the passage) *'The age of miracles no doubt is long passed. They were never meant to continue beyond the first establishment of the church.'* [1]

3. There could be a third way which might appear to be a compromise between the two above. There are many variants of this approach but broadly it entails that we believe that God can and has healed miraculously. We further believe that God is able and willing to do the same today but only does so in highly exceptional instances and that for some dramatic demonstration. Some of us may hover between these three positions at differing stages of our lives. In this context, John Stott differentiates between spiritual gifts and miraculous

---

1. Ryle, J. C., *Expository Thoughts on the Gospels. St. Mark.* James Clarke & Co. Ltd., 1956, p. 362.

gifts. He goes on to reason that the question whether miraculous gifts are bestowed today, cannot be answered with a simple 'yes' or 'no', – for *'I venture to say that the naïve "yes" and "no" answers are both extreme positions.'*[2] To this day it remains difficult to categorise John Stott's position on this debate based on his published views. Perhaps this is as it should be!

Henry Frost, in his book *Miraculous Healing*, written over a century ago, took a similar view,[3] although he shelters behind a semantic argument when he claims, 'There cannot be a recurrence of apostolic miracles – whatever else God may grant – because the apostles as a class have ceased to exist.' He adds a comment that is seldom made nowadays, and which I expect would not be agreeable to Stott – 'When the time comes for a new offering of the kingdom to Israel, miracle-working will be renewed' (Rev. 11:3-6). Like Stott, he took a guarded view on the more general aspects – 'It is my impression that often those persons who have considered the subject of miraculous healing have been extremists, opposing it *in toto* or else endorsing it *in toto,* when neither the one nor the other is justifiable.'

Another aspect of the scriptural understanding of healing arises from the varying interpretations of the nature and extent of the atonement and salvation. Teachers and practitioners of miraculous healing have stressed the fact that *'sozo'* often translated as salvation or deliverance, is used for wholeness, which includes that of physical and mental wholeness or health, as well as in a spiritual sense. Hence it is argued that when Jesus came to 'seek and save the lost' (Luke 19:10), this included a degree of wholeness that is physical. This may be claimed to be an anticipation of the current emphasis on holistic medicine. It has been applied in secular terms in medical practice and in Christian terms by those

2. Stott, J. R., W. *Baptism and Fullness.* IVP, London, 1964, p. 96.
3. Frost, H., *Miraculous Healing.* Evangelical Press, London, 1951, pp. 69, 92, 94.

who appropriate it for divine healing. John Stott deals with this position comprehensively.[4] He agrees that the word *sozo* is used for physical deliverance and for being 'made whole.' But it is also used for deliverance from drowning and from death. People cried to Jesus for deliverance and salvation, and this is how the early church used these stories. 'They believed Jesus had intended them to be illustrations of salvation, not promises of safety or health.' Most tellingly, Peter, having healed the cripple at the temple gate – the man, who had been healed, went on to affirm that 'neither is there salvation in any other name . . . whereby we must be saved' (Acts 4:9-12).

In this aspect again, Frost had anticipated Stott's position. Frost quoted at length from two prominent and highly respected advocates of physical healing being part of the atonement. These were A. J. Gordon and A. B. Simpson. Frost maintains that their interpretations were unjustified from Scripture and falsified by their own life and death experiences, as well as in contemporary history.

Gordon Fee, in his exhaustive work on The Holy Spirit[5] deals in detail with the interrelationship between the body and the Spirit. In his exposition of 1 Corinthians 6:19 – 'your body is the temple of the Holy Spirit', he points out that the Corinthian Christians' understanding of the body amounted to one of disdain. It seemed because they belonged to a heavenly world, there would finally be no body. Paul, in contrast, insisted that the Holy Spirit had everything to do with the body. The body is destined for resurrection. It is, even now, the habitation of the Spirit, so the body also is sanctified by that same Spirit – 'the believer is the present *locus* of God's own *presence.*' The inevitable corollary of this is that just as the sanctified believer is not sinless in this life, so neither is the sanctified body perfectly healthy. This is the corrective against the prevailing Greek dualism that would 'negate the body in favour of the soul.'

4. Stott, J. R. W., *Christian Mission in the Modern World.* Falcon, London, 1975, p. 84.
5. Fee, G. D., *God's Empowering Presence.* Paternoster, UK, 1995, p. 135.

8

Historical and Contemporary Records of Healing

'No testimony is sufficient to establish a miracle unless the testimony be of such a kind that its falsehood would be even more miraculous than the fact which it endeavours to establish' (David Hume).[1]

The above appears in an article 'Demarcation of the Absurd' written by Petr Skrabanek in the *Lancet* in 1986.[2] This is a provocative polemic from a clear-thinking agnostic. Skrabanek is appealing for doctors to use their minds and critical faculties. He upset the medical establishment on several issues that are still relevant. For example, he derided the wholesale institution of various population screening procedures and tests. In this article he attacks bogus healing claims by the medical profession – *'At present, the difference between a doctor and a quack lies not in the nature of their practice but in the possession of a medical diploma'* – hardly the way to win friends and influence the medical establishment! Whilst appealing that the 'absurd' may be dismissed, he also wants the critical faculty to be preserved. He cannot understand how the human mind can hold contradictory positions. For example, the 'incomparable' Isaac Newton could interpret and believe in the prophesies of Daniel and the Apocalypse of St. John. He shares H. L. Menken's bewilderment that the eminent

1. Hume, D., *An inquiry concerning human understanding*. Edited by L. A. Selby-Bigge. Oxford University Press, London, 1902, 115.
2. Skrabanek, P., 'Demarcation of the Absurd'. *Lancet*, 1986, 1:960.

gynaecologist Howard Kelly could believe in Jonah and the whale – '*How is it possible for a human brain to be divided into two insulated halves, one functioning normally, naturally and even brilliantly, and the other capable of ghastly balderdash?*'

I return to this problem below, but if we are Christians, we have to face this issue fairly and squarely, no matter how much we disagree with the way in which such critics deny both God and his word. The fundamental bases of the Christian faith, involving creation of the world, of life and of man, followed by man's redemption through the incarnation of God in Jesus Christ, are absurd to the agnostic and atheist. It then follows that the entire concept of prayer to God and God's direct intervention in human life and affairs is equally untenable. Paul recognised this by describing the gospel as 'foolishness' when faced by the 'wisdom of the world' (1 Corinthians 1:18-25). However, the Christian in turn must not rely on a facile denial in the face of demonstrable facts. Neither must the Christian try to straddle the fence between two extreme positions. Skrabanek ridicules this with his delightful illustration. If there are two claims between 2+2=6 and one of 2+2=4, the truth does not lie in the middle of 2+2=5!

There is a large volume of written records of cases of miraculous healing in the Christian church, dating from the first century. Dr Rex Gardner, in his book on 'Healing Miracles',[3] refers to and summarises a selection of these records from his viewpoint as one who was entirely sympathetic with an acceptance of their reliability. He refers to Martin of Tours (*c.*336-397) and the detailed biography by Clare Stancliffe.[4] The cures claimed were many and various, including three cases of raising the dead.

Following the earlier centuries, claims continued to be made in Britain, for example, such as Cuthbert, King Oswald of Northumbria, John Welch (or Welsh), John Knox's son-in-law

3. Gardner, R., *Healing and Miracles*. Darton, Longman and Todd, London, 1986.
4. Stancliffe, C., *St. Martin and his Hagiographer*. Clarendon Press, Oxford, 1983.

and many others in succeeding centuries. I make no attempt to review these records because I am in no position to assess the evidence in any critical sense, and I cannot accept them in the same way as I accept the biblical records. They have also been described in detail and critically in B. B. Warfield's book.[5]

In the eighteenth and nineteenth centuries miraculous healing was mostly associated with revivals of a charismatic flavour. As these approach our own times and the details of the medical conditions begin to approximate to our own understanding of disease, it may be possible to make some value judgements.

Edward Irving (1792-1834), was an evangelical, Church of Scotland minister, who came to prominence when he became the minister of Regent Square Church in London. His public ministry assumed a strongly charismatic flavour and he stressed the gifts of the Holy Spirit, including that of divine healing. Irving and supporters, who included evangelical Anglicans, went on to form The Catholic Apostolic Church.

Subsequent decades saw the spread of similar movements, emphasising charismatic renewal. At the turn of the century Pentecostalism arose with its further stress on divine healing. This rapidly became a world-wide movement.

Following the Second World War, the general charismatic movement became widespread through all Christian denominational groupings, including the Roman Catholic Church. This has meant that the question of divine miraculous healing has became a prominent feature in all sections of the Christian Church – as well as a cause of dispute and dissension. In some instances this has become more of an issue than the general doctrinal differences between the denominations. This is what has made the debate of great relevance to the beliefs and lives of many Christians today.

---

5. Warfield, B. B., *Counterfeit Miracles.* Banner of Truth Trust, Edinburgh, 1972.

Delusional States

Professing Christians can be deluded. It is vital to recognise this because such people use Christian labels and discredit the true faith.

The *Daily Telegraph* of the 3rd June 1974 reported on a man who claimed to be a convert from one of Billy Graham's London rallies. This man established a cult, the Family Church of Jesus. They met in a terraced house in Great Yarmouth. These people believed they could walk on water and had the gift of healing. They told a Baptist minister at Gorleston, who was crippled, he could be healed immediately. Two of their members drowned, one in the river Yare and the other in the sea, when they went to exercise their 'gifts' by walking on the water. One of these men's wives died two months later. When the police arrived they found her corpse laid out in the living room, surrounded by sect members, who said they were waiting for the woman to be lifted up to heaven.

One of the fascinating aspects of some of the more impossible claims is the way in which delusion can be contagious. *The Times* on 23rd September 1995, reported that frenzied worshippers were converging world-wide on Hindu temples. They believed they could feed their Hindu statues with milk, which the idols drank with gratitude. People flocked to such an extent that the works of government, businesses and schools were disrupted. Scientists were delegated to investigate the phenomenon. According to Hindu mythology such miracles happened when a great soul arrived in the world. The Gods who accepted the milk were Lord Shiva, his consort Parvati, son Ganesh and Nandi his mount. There were reports of devotees flocking to take part in Singapore, the United States, Hong Kong, Indonesia and Bangkok.

I quote this example from a non-Christian source, because it illustrates how evidence needs to be examined critically. In this report, a journalist, Rikee Verma, who states he is a 'religious person,' records that he went to the Hindu temple. He waited with another 200 or so people until his turn came to approach the statue of Ganesh. He placed a spoonful of milk underneath the trunk and within seconds the spoon was empty. He checked the site for leakage or seepage, but concluded there was only one explanation – Ganesh Ji drank the milk. Some other attendees failed because – 'He didn't believe enough in Ganesh.'

The same issue of *The Times* bracketed these reports with those of Roman Catholic claims for weeping statues and blood liquefaction. They also provide exposures of the means by which some of these 'tricks' are worked.

The Times of October 14th 1997, reported the case of a female pastor whose white five-month-old bitch Alsatian dog was hit by a car. The dog lay injured in the road in obvious agony. The pastor prayed over it on the road and refused to call a vet. She and two fellow believers spent almost an hour praying over the dog and speaking in tongues. The pastor said 'Satan get out of this animal.' A neighbour offered help but was told to leave because he was not a Christian. An RSPCA inspector was called. He was told that his fingers were 'instruments of the Devil.' The dog was eventually seized and made a full recovery after having a pin inserted in the broken right front leg. When the owner was tried and found guilty of causing unnecessary pain and suffering, she said that she had a degree in theology from Exeter University and that she had carried out healing missions and had helped blind people to recover their sight. She also said that she was being tried 'for my faith in the healing powers of the Lord Jesus Christ.'

I quote this case as an illustration how commonsense may desert people whilst they claim justification for their words and actions in the name of Christianity and Jesus Christ. Such events have the flavour of an absence of rational thinking if not of frank delusional states.

There are many other near-contemporary records of cults who have claimed to exorcise demons, drink poisons, killing of individuals and mass suicides – all in the name of God and Christianity. When we know of such bizarre claims, I believe we need to be unafraid to be clear. Such developments are, at best, the result of delusional states, or at worst, of devilish origin. When Paul wrote to his young friend Timothy, he warned of all sorts of heresies, perversions and sheer criminality. One of the gifts given by God in these circumstances was that of a 'sound mind' (2 Timothy 1:7). We should not be afraid of a charge of intellectualism or rationality. God has given his believers minds and good sense. We need to exercise the same. The Christian is, by definition, a person of faith. Furthermore, the expression of that faith will to the man of the world appear to be foolishness. However, there is no call to be frankly ridiculous.

The Missionary Scene

It may be generally assumed in Christian circles that evidence of miraculous divine healing is more impressive in missionary situations in developing or Third World countries. These are usually against a background of relative poverty and lack of education and modern medical services. Such societies have a younger population and a shorter life-expectancy. These settings mean that it is more difficult to satisfy any criteria that might be imposed to substantiate the claims that are made. This, of course, does not invalidate such claims but makes them less compelling. I take a few typical examples which may illustrate both the problem and possibly a challenge to the Western way of thinking.

Dr Kurt Koch, in his account of 'The Revival in Indonesia'[6,7] tells of how, prior to the revival on the island of Timor, a teacher received a vision in October 1964. This man was told to proceed to Timor and hold a healing mission there. The area was one where sorcerers were prominent and where the occult was prevalent. The man, Jephthah, proceeded to heal all who came to him. Several thousand people were healed and these miracles were said to have been authenticated by a local church mission committee. Many individual and mass examples of healing are then recorded. These include a resurrection five hours after death.

---

6. Koch, K., *The Revival in Indonesia*. Evangelisation Publishers, Western Germany.
7. ────── *Wine of God*. Christian Evangelisation Publications, Canada, 1974.

In one case a child had been dead for two days when the parents, instead of burying the child, according to custom on the first day of death, waited a further two days, and called for the mother. After some prayer time the child was restored to life.

Koch pointed out that, at the time, there were practically no doctors at all on Timor and the neighbouring islands. The sick would seek help from village sorcerers. There was a very strong occult background. He records individual cases. 'Saul' developed sudden blindness. Sight was restored after 'Saul' had a vision of Jesus Christ and had obeyed the command to hand over some fetishes which he kept at home in a case. This same 'Saul', in turn, became a healer, which included the resurrection of a nine-year-old boy.

In October 1972 the Overseas Missionary Fellowship circulated a report on *The 'Revival' in Timor*. This was written by Dr Frank L. Cooley, a theologian and missionary. He returned to Timor for six weeks to investigate and evaluate the nature of the revival and its claims. He interviewed extensively, using the Indonesian language when appropriate. All previous writers, including Dr Kurt Koch, had worked through interpreters. Much of Dr Cooley's report concerns the nature of the revival and its effects on the native populations and Christian church in the islands. He also, as in the case of Dr Koch, emphasises the primitive conditions of life in these islands at that time. Religion was often of an animistic nature. People had no one to turn to during sickness other than to their own 'spiritual healers.' Dr Cooley concluded: *'It is impossible to check this (i.e. miraculous healing claims) in any scientific fashion. There is no doubt in my mind that a great many people did experience what they considered to be miracles through the ministry of the teams. Many of these healings took place in people burdened by emotional, guilt problems related to the general spiritual atmosphere of Timorese society. Liberating people by the power of the Gospel from the burden of guilt and fear believing that they are under a curse, undoubtedly carries with it liberation from physical and emotional symptoms. A large percentage of the healings reported to me were of this nature. Perhaps it is an open question whether these should be called miracles.'*

Dr Cooley then dealt with the miracles that had been so widely and spectacularly reported, such as, the changing of water into communion wine, restoration of sight and hearing, walking on water and the raising the dead. He failed to confirm these and found it impossible for an investigator to draw a clear distinction between the objective and subjective dimensions in a particular case. He fairly allows that even amongst Christian interpreters it appeared to depend on your previous theological orientation. He did, however, interview a man whose wife had been claimed to be raised from the dead following the burning of images in a Roman Catholic Church. This man confirmed that the healing team had tried to restore her to life but had failed.

Diarmaid MacCulloch in his magisterial *A History of Christianity*,[8] deals with this cultural problem – *'At the heart of Christianity is a book full of signs and wonders testifying to God's power, and Africans were accustomed to looking for these . . . in fact, Africans might take the book more seriously than the missionaries who brought it, in the sense that they expected concrete results from the power of God. That was a challenge to European Evangelicals, who were likewise convinced that God wrought miracles in his world, but whose rationalism (born at whatever remove from the Enlightenment) provoked them into alarm at a literalism which differed from their own.'* MacCulloch writes as an historian and describes his position as a 'candid friend of Christianity.' He certainly does not take an evangelical standpoint. Nevertheless, I find his summary of the dilemma which may face an evangelical both fair and compelling.

Claims in the Western and Developed Nations

Dr Rex Gardner, referred to above, wrote an article in the *British Medical Journal*, the title of which gives a flavour – *'Miracles of healing in Anglo-Celtic Northumbria as recorded by the Venerable*

---

8. MacCulloch, Diarmaid, *A History of Christianity. The First Three Thousand Years.* Allen Lane, London, 2009, p. 882.

Bede and his contemporaries: a reappraisal in the light of twentieth century experience.' [9] In this, to me most confusing article, Gardner appears to seek to authenticate miracles of healing attributed to Bede, Cuthbert and their contemporaries, by recording comparable case histories of miraculous healing in a modern setting. The trouble is that these modern examples are themselves wide open to alternative explanations. It would be tedious to analyse each in turn, but I would simply emphasise that there were significant medical interventions in five of them. Gardner describes seven cases. The seventh case was that of a return to life twenty minutes after death in a woman of around 50 years in a missionary setting in North Thailand. Gardner himself concludes that: *'No attempt has been made to prove that miracles have occurred, such proof being probably impossible.'*

Dr Peter May[10] has investigated the above. He has also granted me sight of correspondence between himself and Dr Gardner which, in my view, confirms the unsatisfactory nature of the medical evidence provided in an attempt to claim miraculous healing. May also provides several other specific and near contemporary examples.

1. Esmond Jefferies in his book, *The Power and the Glory*, describes the miracles of healing that featured at Pin Mill in Suffolk. Prominent aspects included the use of hypnotism, relaxation, laying on of hands on the diseased part of the body and visualisation of the destruction of cancer cells. Dr May focussed on two of the claimed miracles. In one, a man had an unusual sarcoma which was treated with radical chemotherapy and radiotherapy – which surely vitiated any independent evaluation. In

9. Gardner, R., 'Miracles of Healing in Anglo-Catholic Northumbria as recorded by the Venerable Bede and his contemporaries: a reappraisal in the light of twentieth century experience'. *BMJ*, 1983, 287:1927.

10. May, P., Several personal communications, including his address to the General Synod, July 1991; an Open Letter to Dr Rex Gardner, 5th December 1994, with replies; text of lecture to the Victoria Institute, 18th October 2007, and accounts of Jennifer Rees Larcombe.

another case there was a claim of instantaneous recovery of hearing. Further authentication proved impossible. In addition, such events have been well reported without any involvement of a miraculous element.

2. Dr May summarised his experience and research in this field in his lecture given to the Victoria Institute on 18th October 2007. He scathingly exposes charlatans who peddle false hope to sick people, and often make fortunes from doing so. Dr May also provides useful guidelines in the definition of a miracle of healing in the New Testament use of the word. Gospel miracles were exhibited for conditions that were non-remitting and incurable; they were instantaneous; they were complete and no other therapy was provided.

One of the most revealing aspects of Dr May's investigations in this field was his account of attempting to validate the facts in cases of claimed healing. This was illustrated in his dealings with Morris Cerullo who proved elusive when Dr May sought to chase the facts. Similar difficulties were found when he investigated the 22 claims of healing in Dr Rex Gardner's book. In fact, he found, on follow-up that two of these patients had died from their diseases in the same year that his book was published.

In 1992, BBC1 transmitted two programmes in the 'Heart of the Matter' series, presented by Joan Bakewell. These examined the Morris Cerullo campaign. Dr May contributed to the BBC production. He was especially concerned with the accompanying large print message, 'Have faith and abandon your medication.' This was highlighted by the Southwark coroner, Sir Montague Levine, who castigated this message at the inquest he conducted into the death of a 25-year-old woman. This lady stopped her drug treatment for epilepsy after attending a meeting held by Cerullo at Earl's Court. Six days later she drowned in her bath.

In 1991 Dr May investigated the claims of Jennifer Rees Larcombe, as shown on ITV ('The Human Factor', Sunday, 17th

November 1991) and in published books. The diagnosis in her case varied from a recurrent viral encephalitis to chronic myalgic encephalomyelitis (ME). Again Dr May experienced the greatest difficulty in verification and deplored the false hope engendered for those suffering from other diseases of the nervous system such as Alzheimer's dementia, Huntingdon's Chorea, Motor Neurone Disease and Multiple Sclerosis.

Dr May concludes that: *'I have searched in vain for over forty years for compelling evidence of a contemporary miraculous healing.'* He also recounts his personal difficulty in having his book *Looking for a Miracle* published. *'Publishers tell me this book should certainly be published – but not by them!'*

Dr William A. Nolen published in 1975 the results of his investigations into the claims of Kathryn Kuhlman.[11,12] He even volunteered as an usher in one of her miracle services. After exhaustive inquiry he concluded: *'After doing my best for eighteen months to find some shred of evidence that somewhere there was someone who had miraculous healing powers, I concluded that no such person existed.'*

Dr Brad Burke,[13] similarly examined near contemporary claims. He analysed the claims made by Benny Hinn, Oral Roberts, Reinhard Bonnke (all of whom claim to have raised the dead), Pat Roberts and others. His exposé is devastating. Like others, as above, he reports several instances when attempts to validate claims were obstructed or ignored. He also quotes the claims by leaders in the Vineyard movement of a woman instantly growing a new breast following mastectomy; a previously blind, paralysed girl, jumping up with her legs and sight recovered; teeth and fillings turned to gold – *'all without a shred of credible, external evidence.'*

11. Nolen, W. A., *Healing: A Doctor in Search of a Miracle*. Random House, New York, 1975, pp. 208, 228.
12. Kuhlman, K., *I Believe in Miracles*. Prentice-Hall, Englewood Cliffs, N.J., 1969.
13. Burke, B., *Does God Still Do Miracles?*. Victor Kingsway Communications, Eastbourne, 2006.

Oral Roberts, who died at the age of 91 on 15th December 2009, was described in a *Daily Telegraph* obituary (17th December 2009) as the doyen of American televangelists. At the risk of being accused of personalising the issue, Oral Roberts's life provides a telling critique of the twentieth century charismatic healing movement. Roberts placed his miraculous healing powers at the centre of his ministry. He claimed that God had spoken to him 'take My healing power to your generation.' His claims of healing ranged from haemorrhoids to cancer. During his televised performances he would place his healing hand against the lens of the camera whilst instructing the sufferer to place his or her hand on the television screen. At the same time a request would be made for '*seed faith*' *donations – 'twenty dollars, Visa, Amex, whatever the Lord leads you to do.*' Another of his methods was to receive daily, thick, typed lists of sufferers which Roberts would pray over. All this was accompanied by the raising of vast sums of money, at one stage grossing $110 million per year, the establishment of the Oral Roberts University, a City of Faith medical complex with 777 beds (which became insolvent), and an elaborate base in Tulsa, Oklahoma.

The Independent obituary of Oral Roberts on 17th December 2009 makes the ironic observation that disabled people were excluded from the campus until the American Civil Liberties Union brought a successful anti-discrimination suit!

The obituaries also describe Roberts's own extravagant life-style. I am conscious of the danger of basing any argument on the life of any individual, but, in this case at least, I maintain that the entire picture is so remote from what we read of Jesus, his disciples and the New Testament church that it serves to condemn what is but a travesty of gospel truth.

There are many instances where healing claims are so farcical that they have their amusing aspect. Professor Verna Wright (in 'CMF Guidelines', Number 98) describes one such – '*At Horsforth, on the edge of Leeds, Don Double conducted a healing crusade. He claims to heal different ailments on various nights. One night he was healing the deaf, and a friend of mine who is deaf in one ear thought he would like to be healed. Hands were laid upon him and he was told that he was healed. He replied, "I am not". The healer said, "Yes you are". "No, I am not", my friend insisted; only to be told, "Well it must be that you don't have sufficient faith". After a brief altercation the healer went down the line of deaf people. When the healing activities had finished, my friend turned to the lady next to him and said, "What did it do for you, love?" She replied with her hand cupped to her ear, "What did you say?!"'*

Father Francis MacNutt

One of the most influential people in the charismatic healing movement during the last century has been Francis MacNutt. He was a Professor of Homiletics and one of the first Catholics involved in the charismatic renewal. His book on *Healing*[14] was first published in 1974 and is still read and quoted by Christians of many denominations. This book is both highly personal and anecdotal. Therefore, it is difficult to summarise the book in a systematic manner. All I can do is to take examples of his methods and claims. The difficulty is compounded by the way in which MacNutt quotes other claims uncritically without any additional comment.

MacNutt refers to the reports from Rev. Franklin Loehr, a chemist, who recorded that 156 persons praying in 700 unit experiments using more than 27,000 seeds involving some 100,000 measurements, achieved up to a 52.71% growth advantage.

In the same context MacNutt quotes the work of Dr Bernard Grad in which he found that wound healing in mice, as well as the growth of rye grass, were speeded up when prayed for at a distance of 600 miles. I confess that I have not tried to trace and read these references for myself!

Although MacNutt admits that experiments such as the above 'have an element of the bizarre,' this does not dissuade him from

---

14. MacNutt, F., *Healing*. Ave Maria Press, Indiana, 1974.

using their claims in support of his general argument in favour of the miraculous.

I read MacNutt's book looking for evidence that would support his claims, but so often found, instead, examples such as the above. These recur throughout – for example, *'. . . our cat has coughing spells that really irritate us. We've prayed and laid hands on her, cast off bad spirits, etc. Veterinary bills are expensive and since we will not allow sickness in our lives, why allow it in our cat's life?'* I find the 'etc' intriguing! No wonder that he says that *'many of these healings taken individually are ambiguous as proof; they can be explained in a variety of ways.'* They certainly can. It gives no cause for satisfaction to quote such ridiculous examples.

I admit that reactions to stories similar to these are personal and conditioned by our own training and attitudes. It may well be that I am too ready to discount supernatural explanations when there could be a perfectly natural and explicable one. Thus, by background, I find it difficult to accept the role of relics in this field. Therefore, I begin to question when even a mainline Anglican, like Rev. Michael Green, in his book *I believe in Satan's downfall*,[15] claims that miracles of healing may be aided by the use of crucifixes. He recounts that when dealing with a person under the influence of multiple demon possession, he had no 'holy water.' The afflicted person challenged him 'Ah, you haven't got any holy water.' Green replied, 'I have.' Green proceeded to consecrate some water in a glass in the name of the Trinity and used it to sprinkle the woman. He says *'The effect was immediate, electric and amazing. She jumped as if she had been scalded.'* May I be forgiven if my cynical and incredulous reaction is one that denotes a lack of faith, but I still believe that the whole tone of such stories speaks to me of the realm of magicians or Harry Potter. How different from the entire atmosphere that accompanied Jesus' miracles of healing.

I suspect that a person's response to the use of relics is not always, or even often, a reflection of one's religious belief. Melanie

---

15. Green, M., *I Believe in Satan's Downfall.* Hodder & Stoughton, London, 1981.

McDongah, writing as a journalist (*Daily Telegraph*, 21.9.09) used the occasion of the tour of the relics of St. Therese of Liseux, to attack the 'secularism' of Protestantism. This was in response to Simon Jenkins's dismissal of relics as 'jujus, religious placebos for the credulous classes.' McDonagh classes the failure to venerate relics as equivalent to the atheism of Richard Dawkins. She then tries to confirm her views by referring to Lourdes *'littered with discarded crutches and we can argue the toss about whether it's the result of psychosomatic healing or divine help.'* Then she adds to give credence to her claims *'a remarkable number of those miracles of healing have been independently verified by doctors with no church connections. And that's a fact.'* It is not a fact. Kenneth L. Woodward, writing in 2000,[16] reported that since the first miraculous cure was recorded in 1858, *'only 66 of 6,000 healing claims'* have been *'authenticated by the shrine's medical boards.'* Dr Brad Burke[17] reports that only four healing miracles have been accepted in the past four decades and even these have been criticised by medical professionals.

Lourdes
The above will appear as a fundamental criticism of Lourdes, but this is not my purpose. I am simply trying to apply the same criteria as I would apply to any claim for miraculous healing. The ministry of Lourdes may have other more significant validity on a different level. This is well illustrated in the case of Abigail Witchells, who was stabbed in the neck in a motiveless attack, which left her paralysed.[18] She first went to Lourdes as a healthy 19-year-old. This was, in her words, as a 'spectator.' When she returned eight years later in 2006, in her wheelchair, she saw it from the inside as a 'pilgrim.' She had already prayed for healing, but now she prayed: *'Heal me in the way I need most, according to your will.'* She went on to say how God did answer this prayer –

---

16. Woodward, K. L., *The Book of Miracles,* Simon and Schuster, New York, 2000.
17. Burke, B., *Does God Still Do Miracles?*. Victor Communications, Eastbourne, 2006.
18. Witchalls, A., *The Daily Telegraph*, 30th April 2009, p. 29.

not physically, but He did free her to love life. This enabled her to give more as a paralysed person than when she was able-bodied. This is precisely the long-standing testimony of paraplegic Joni Eareckson Tada. Catherine Simon in her biography of Abigail Witchell's experience of Lourdes, writes: *'Now . . . I know the beginnings of what faith truly tastes like, what pain resembles and what wonders God can achieve.'*[19]

As soon as I read Abigail Witchall's compelling testimony, I obtained the book to which she refers. The book is written in a discursive style which makes it difficult to assess. Eight of the cases describe people with severe paralysis, acute myeloid leukaemia, severe encephalitis, multiple sclerosis, Asperger's syndrome and cerebral palsy. None of these experienced healing of their medical condition. The accounts stress the spiritual healing which took place – both in the case of the 'patients' and particularly amongst those close to them as well as their carers.

In all the above I have studied the medical evidence as impartially as I can. As far as is humanly possible I have tried to assess the claims and criticisms as neutrally as I can – in fact, it would have been a relief to find incontrovertible 'proof' of instantaneous miraculous, physical healing in response to prayer akin to the miracles recorded in the Bible. I have failed to find such. This does not mean that they did not occur or that the claims were false or deliberately misleading. All I could conclude is that even if the healings were precisely as narrated, the events could be explicable on grounds of natural history, remission, mistaken diagnosis, insufficient follow-up, psychosomatic or placebo effect, etc. However, the ninth case quoted is in a different category.

The case of Jean-Pierre Bely. *I wish to consider this case in greater detail as it exemplifies the dilemma we face as we seek to understand. This man, born in 1936, qualified as a nurse and worked in intensive care. He and his wife lived as*

19. Simon, C., *Where Echoes Meet. Nine Lives Changed by Lourdes.* Three Peaks Press, Abergavenny, 2008.

traditional Catholics. In 1972 he lost consciousness and had an episode of double vision. He recovered quickly but then had 'several episodes of illness.' In October 1984 he became paralysed on his left side. He was told that his illness 'resembles multiple sclerosis.' Further tests were performed in hospital. No firmer diagnosis was given, but he was told that he would have to 'make do with it.' The degree of disability fluctuated. Sometimes he could not walk and began to use a wheelchair.

The family visited Lourdes many times. In 1987, at the age of 51 they went as usual. Between the 3rd to 9th October, Jean-Pierre had an intense spiritual experience with a vision of a woman in white. He received the sacrament of Anointing. He then experienced a variety of sensations; a return of feeling in his hands and fingers; hears a call to get up and walk and eventually does so. His physical improvement was dramatic. Muscles which had not functioned for a long time were normal 'in a few weeks.' When he arrived home and saw his usual doctor, he was told that it might have been a crowd phenomenon or the atmosphere in Lourdes. No plausible explanation could be found. A specialist neurologist also found the transformation inexplicable.

Jean-Pierre subsequently received much publicity. In 1989 he visited Pope John Paul II at the Vatican. He was examined by the Medical Bureau of Lourdes and after a process of eleven years and multiple medical examinations his case was recognised by the Church as a sign from God, a miracle. The conclusion of Dr Patrick Theiller, Doctor in Charge of the Medical Bureau, is quoted – 'It is possible to conclude, with a good margin of probability, that M. Bely suffered an organic infection of the multiple sclerosis type in a severe and advanced stage, of which the sudden cure during a pilgrimage to Lourdes corresponds with an unusual and inexplicable fact with regard to science. It is impossible to say anything more today. It is for the religious authorities, however, to make a pronouncement on the other dimensions of this cure.'

In 1997, Jean-Pierre's wife developed breast cancer which was treated with surgery and radical chemotherapy.

In 2005, Jean-Pierre developed cancer of the liver and 'suffered terribly in the last months.' He returned to Lourdes in October 2005. He came home where he died on 27th October with his wife at his side.

The full account should be read in Catherine Simon's book, but this abstract should be enough to show the wide variety of reactions which M. Bely's life may provoke. These can be considered on differing levels.

On a medical level, there is no doubt that Bely suffered from severe disability, reducing him to a wheelchair and at times a stretcher. It is also clear that these physical problems more or less disappeared in a dramatic fashion. However, the primary diagnosis remains doubtful. His symptoms were consistent with a diagnosis of multiple sclerosis. But his doctors had some reservations, in that they concluded that his illness 'resembled' multiple sclerosis. Following his 'cure', Dr Theiller referred to 'an organic infection of the multiple sclerosis type.' These guarded and qualified statements suggest the diagnosis was not incontrovertible. Multiple sclerosis may present in a wide variety of ways making diagnosis difficult and often delayed or mistaken.

Not only may the diagnosis be difficult or mistaken, so also may the course of the disease. Many patients are seen in which the disease fluctuates unpredictably. Dramatic remission may occur. The standard *Oxford Textbook of Medicine*, for example, states that patients 'may remain symptom-free for many years or may recover spontaneously from severe paralysis.' This unpredictability is such a feature of the disease, that it makes it very difficult to assess the therapeutic action of any drug treatment.

For these reasons, based on the medical evidence as provided, I believe the claim for miraculous physical healing in Bely's case, is not beyond a significant element of doubt. I believe the medical evidence is not proven.

On a practical human level, what are we to make of the subsequent history with the development of liver cancer which was untreatable medically and unresponsive to a Lourdes pilgrimage. This is hardly a sensible objection. After all, the most ardent advocate of divine miraculous intervention does not claim the gift of immortality. Even Lazarus, having been raised from the dead by Jesus, would die in due time.

On a spiritual level, a much more compelling case is being made. Simon comments in her book, 'John-Pierre, however, never liked to think of his cure as a miracle, but as a sign from God or a healing . . . he considered, however, that the word "miracle" was used in far too many contexts and that Jesus himself had never talked of a miracle, only signs.' His own wife urged upon him: 'You have to explain to people that there are miracles that take place which are invisible, in the heart.' Simon concludes: 'Jean-Pierre left the healing of his body behind him in a coffin, left to decay and crumble. He carried his interior healing with him into eternity.' Those that saw him in his terminal illness from cancer all recognised his faith in Christ and in his resurrection. Who can object to or criticise such comments?

This type of difficulty in interpreting the happenings at Lourdes has been present from its inception. Alexis Carrel (1873-1944), who was awarded the Nobel Prize for his work on tissue culture, was a rationalist who was converted as a result of what he saw at Lourdes. He visited there, as a sceptic, in 1903. A manuscript was found after his death and published in 1950 as *The Journey to Lourdes*. (Quoted by Dr Theodore Dalrymple in the *BMJ*: 339:b3982.) A girl, Marie Ferrand had tuberculosis. Both her parents had died from the disease. She developed severe tuberculous peritonitis. Carrel examined her shortly before she visited the Lourdes grotto and concluded she would die very soon. However, within a few minutes of arriving at the grotto the peritonitis disappeared. Dalrymple goes on to tell of his own experience 'in a distant country', when similar cases responded dramatically to laparotomy – 'letting the air in.' What are we to make of such accounts? Dalrymple faces the issue, the title of his article being 'Now I'm a believer', by asking – 'An old wives' tale? I doubt that a double blind trial has ever been done. But if it was, and the results were negative, I should continue to believe in "letting the air in". Like Carel, I have faith.' I simply do not know how to react to such accounts. The obvious way is to accept, both Carrel's and Dalrymple's versions as descriptions of miracles. Certainly, they were 'signs', which in Carrel's case seem to have converted him to the Christian faith. Dalrymple also asserts that he has faith, but he does not specify the nature of his faith. It could be read that he had faith in 'letting the air in.' I must also comment, as a pathologist, that the diagnosis in the case of Marie Ferrand, although highly suggestive, is based on circumstantial evidence. We lack the medical details and the proof of the presence of tuberculous peritonitis. Even Nobel prize-winners could be mistaken if their diagnosis were based on superficial examination!

The case of Canon David Watson is one that highlights many of the difficulties in assessing faith healing. A routine medical check uncovered cancer which proved to be inoperable and had spread to the liver. He was given six months to a year, or maybe two years, to live. Three American ministers flew from America and prayed with him for three days. One of these said: 'I believe that the root of this cancer has been cut and soon it will begin to die.' Watson said: 'As I prayed I just felt the power of God in my body. It felt 500% better and positively began to believe I was being healed.'[20] Watson published a book shortly before he died in February 1984.[21] In a highly perceptive review of this book in the *Journal of The Christian Medical Fellowship* (1984), Dr Peter Pattison, summarises: 'Let us not despise the positive emphases that have come in many aspects of the twentieth century healing movement. However, we need to ask if God is not in this book and through this life calling us on both sides of the Atlantic back to the historic values of the Christian faith that see time and

20. Watson, D., *Your are my God*. Hodder and Stoughton, London, 1984.
21. ———— *Fear No Evil*. ———————— ————, 1984.

eternity, natural and supernatural as all of a piece in the providence of God?' Pattison also refers to a quote from a grossly disfigured Ugandan Christian, 'God never promises us an easy time. Just a safe arrival.'

I end this chapter with an example of the stark contrast between literally incredible claims with that of a real life example of a consecrated Christian life. Both Rex Gardiner and Francis McNutt, quoted above, refer approvingly to instances amongst Sioux Indians at Blue Cloud Abbey (Marvin, South Dakota) where people miraculously received dental fillings, of silver or gold, some of which assumed a cruciform outline. I compare such accounts with the later years of pioneer missionary C. T. Studd.[22] This formerly wealthy English test cricketer, now living out his final years in a primitive hut in central Africa, was greatly troubled with his few remaining teeth. He quoted in parody the poet who summarised his dental problem as *'Gums, gums everywhere but not a sign of teeth!'* He was urged by local Christians to return to England for dental treatment. Studd's reply was to the effect that if God willed him to have new teeth he would see to it. In the event a dentist, Mr Buck, who was too old to be accepted by the Heart of Africa Mission, sold his practice and made his way to the Congo. Mr Buck made enough money on arrival to fund his further journey inland to make a two-week river journey to find C. T. Studd. When the two men met, Mr Buck extracted his few teeth and fitted him with dentures. Studd summarised the story – 'Just fancy God sending a dentist to the very Heart of Africa to look after the teeth of His child, who could not return home. What wonder will God not do next?' Can we imagine this laconic, quintessential Englishman dreaming that God would insert silver/gold fillings in a cruciform shape?

---

22. Grub, Norman, *C. T. Studd*. Lutterworth Press, London, 1970, p. 228.

9.

Why Pray?

'I do not think that a petition which misses the mind of God will ever be answered' (J. O. Fraser).[1]

Having cast a critical look at some aspects of recent claims made by Christians for miraculous healing, I stop and question where such scepticism may lead us. If, for the sake of argument, we conclude that, in general, miracles of healing do not occur in direct answer to prayer, what of the rest of life? What then is the point of praying? This is a challenge repeatedly made by those who are not Christians.

Do we conclude that our lives are governed by natural law only? Is the possibility of divine intervention a mere wish? Is there any point in praying to God in a crisis – whether personal, national or within the church itself?

If we follow this route we are left with a belief and a life which is lived entirely on a natural plane, with no supernatural element. Such a life may or may not be guided by a moral code or an ethical system. This position leaves us with a huge question mark, not only on our own lives, but also over the supernatural nature of the claims of the entire biblical revelation. It also challenges me immediately whenever I exercise my own critical faculty in connection with any miraculous claim. If I should reject many of these claims, what right have I to assert and depend on God's guidance, protection and ultimately salvation in my own life? This is an issue that has to be faced on a personal level.

---

1. Fraser, J. O. (Mrs.), *Fraser and Prayer.* Overseas Missionary Fellowship, London, 1963, p. 32.

I confess I have listened and read claims made by Christians of incredible 'answers to prayer' and found that I react with disbelief to some of them. When I take such a stance I am reminded of A. W. Tozer's writing *In Praise of Disbelief*.[2] In a world that is even more gullible and superstitious than when Tozer wrote, it is refreshing to read: *'Credulity, on the other hand, never honors God, . . . The credulous person will accept anything as long as it is unusual, and the more unusual it is the more ardently will he believe . . . The gullible mentality is like the ostrich, that will gulp down anything that looks interesting – an orange, a tennis ball, a pocketknife opened or closed, a paper weight or a ripe apple. That he survives at all is a testimony not to his intelligence but to his tough constitution.'* He goes on to say that he has met Christians *'with no more discrimination than the ostrich. Because they must believe certain things, they feel they must believe everything. Because they are called upon to accept the invisible they go right on to accept the incredible.'* When I read such words I feel re-assured. They have the ring of good sense. But then I check myself. There is always the danger of reinforcing natural scepticism, so that the truly miraculous may be dismissed.

This parallels the entire problem with miraculous healing. It may well depend on our own personal predilections and attitudes. The credulous may need to be reminded of Tozer, whereas as someone like me needs to be challenged with the charge of faithlessness. Furthermore, gullibility is not confined to the Christian. Superstition has been rife amongst unbelievers before, and since G. K. Chesterton, wrote: *'When people stop believing in God, they don't believe in nothing – they believe in anything.'*

The Centenary Memorial publication of George Muller's *Autobiography*[3] consists of 736 closely-typed pages, the bulk of which is taken up with the countless ways in which Muller's and the prayers of his co-workers were answered precisely and repeatedly, so that the needs of thousands of orphans in England

2. Tozer, A. W., *The Root of the Righteous*. Christian Publications, Inc., Harrisburg, P.A. 1955, p. 119.
3. Muller, G., *Autobiography*. J. Nisbet and Co., London, 1914.

should be met. What presumption it would be for anyone, Christian or unbeliever, to question or criticise such a life lived in faith. Following Muller's death at the age of 93 years on the 10th March 1898, further evidence emerged what that life entailed. His successor, James Wright, found frequent entries of gifts from 'a servant of the Lord Jesus, who constrained by the love of Christ, seeks to lay up treasure in heaven.' This servant was none other than Muller himself who had given an aggregate sum of £81,490 pounds, 18 shillings and 8 pence from money given to him for himself. There were many other gifts separate from those used for the upkeep of the orphanages. When he died his personal estate amounted to £169.9s.4d.[4]

It could be argued, even by those who accept the evidence of a life as momentous as that of George Muller's, that such a life is highly exceptional – in the same way as healing miracles may be. That is obviously true, but what of the countless individual examples of incidents? For example, Colin Duriez in his biography of Francis Schaeffer[5] refers to a conversation he had with Schaeffer's widow, Edith. The Schaeffers were contemplating the purchase of a chalet in Switzerland. The chalet would be for their work amongst young people and would also be part of their appeal against deportation from the country. Time was running out. They prayed specifically 'send us a sign . . . send us 1,000 dollars before ten o'clock tomorrow morning.' The next morning's mail included a letter: 'Tonight we have come to a definite decision, and both of us feel certain that we are meant to send you this money . . . to buy a house somewhere that will always be open to young people.' The letter contained a cheque for exactly one thousand dollars. As the purchase of the house proceeded, the exact amounts were sent and permission was granted for the Schaeffers to remain in Switzerland. When we are confronted by stories of this nature, where the events are beyond coincidence, we can either believe them or accuse their authors of lying.

---

4. Miller, B., *George Muller. Man of Faith and Miracles.* Zondervan, Dimension Books, Minnesota, 1941.
5. Duriez, C., *Francis Schaeffer; An Authentic Life.* IVP, Nottingham, 2008.

The only conclusion I can reach is that, even laying aside the scriptural evidence, it is clear that God is alive. He hears and answers prayer. Having said that, I immediately admit there are so many examples where our lives and those of others may pursue their humdrum courses, including times of great pain and tragedy, where our prayers are not answered in the way we desire and when the heavens 'seem as brass.' This is precisely the contradiction we find in the case of miraculous healing as compared with our common experiences of disease and illness. The apparent contradiction does not, of itself, invalidate the miraculous.

There cannot have been a more distinguished and dedicated Christian doctor in the last century than Dr Paul Brand. His long life was devoted to the study of disease and the alleviation of patients suffering from leprosy. Dr Brad Burke[6] wrote to him shortly before he died, asking him if he had ever seen a miracle of healing. He replied: *'I have not experienced (or recognised, perhaps) a miracle of healing . . . one that requires an alteration of the laws of nature.'* Burke goes on to write that following his own thank-you letter to Dr Brand, he received unexpectedly a follow-up letter from Dr Brand, emphasising the power of prayer – *'I have no doubts whatever that as we pray the Holy Spirit does help the sick individual to experience positive changes in his outlook and to face his sickness – or even his death – in a way that is healthy and that helps him to utilize physical resources and mental and emotional resources which are profoundly useful in developing health and either in postponing death or making it into a positive experience.'* Here, surely, is an answer to 'Why pray?' that has the ring of authenticity. Dr Brand's interpretation could be regarded as the 'Protestant' version of Abigail Witchell's experience at Catholic Lourdes!

All this becomes part, not so much of our understanding of disease, illness and healing, but rather how we react and cope with it when it affects us or those we know and love. This is the subject of our next chapter.

---

6. Burke, B., ibid.

10.

The Heavens are as Brass

'It would be strange to suppose that mankind was redeemed by the sufferings of the Saviour, to live in ease and softness themselves; that suffering should be necessary atonement for sin and yet that sinners should be excused from sufferings.'
(William Law, *Christian Perfection*, 1726).

Whichever position we take on the matter of miraculous divine healing, we are left with the problem of unanswered prayer; of innocent suffering; of unrelieved pain and the inevitability of death.

If physical, not to mention material well-being, is included in the atonement, we have to deny that good people suffer and die – or that the atonement never applied to them in the first place. This attitude is not far removed from the statement that any failure to obtain miraculous healing is due to a lack of faith on the part of the sick person. I find such a view as absurd as it is cruel. Do we say this when a child of 3 years develops a fulminating cancer that does not respond to treatment – regardless of what the parents may, or may not, believe?

Biblical Examples
Everyone in the Bible, apart from Enoch and Elijah, died, either from natural causes, or accident, or were killed. This includes those, in both Old and New Testament, who were 'raised from the dead.'

The way in which we read, interpret and use the Bible is a good illustration in itself of how we can belong to one camp or another in respect of miraculous healing. We may, on the one hand, concentrate on the supernatural accounts of divine intervention in cases of disease and death. On the other hand we may emphasise the instances where lives are lived 'normally', when people are born, live and die on a perfectly natural basis. At this juncture I wish to do the latter.

It should be self-evident, but yet I suggest this needs emphasising – namely, that the overwhelming majority of people in scriptural times lived lives on a biological level, during which they experienced health, sickness and death patterns, which were ordinary and natural. Furthermore, we do not see that these experiences were significantly different depending on whether they believed in God or not. Miracles were recorded for this reason. They were exceptional and noteworthy.

If we concentrate on the New Testament records, there is no suggestion that Christians were healthier or lived longer than their compatriots. They all died in due course. Some had chronic illness. Timothy had some sickness that showed as 'asthenia' affecting his 'stomach'. The nature of this sickness is a matter for conjecture. All we know is that Paul advised him not to drink water but to resort to a 'little wine' (1 Timothy 5:23). Strangely enough this advice is still sometimes given to travellers in countries where the water supplies are unreliable. There is no account of Timothy's clinical response. We may wonder why Paul did not resort to prayer for his healing – or possibly he did pray without any improvement in Timothy's condition.

Paul himself provides an even more striking example. In 1 Corinthians 12:7-10, he speaks feelingly of the way in which Satan used illness to cut him down to size – 'lest I should be exceedingly uplifted.' This 'thorn in the flesh' was presumably a painful and chronic condition. We can only guess as to its precise diagnosis. Surely Paul, the great intercessor, will have prayed repeatedly for cure or alleviation. He specifies that he prayed on three occasions for healing. We may well wonder as to the intensity of these prayers. It is even reminiscent of Jesus praying three times in the garden that the fate of crucifixion might be averted. In our way of thinking we could have claimed how cure would release us for greater service. Paul could have pointed out how his missionary journeys would have been facilitated if he did not have his affliction.

Paul was not cured. There is no record that his condition was even alleviated. We do know Paul received something far greater. God spoke to him. The words given are left imperishably, not only for Paul, but for the countless believers who have claimed them in times of trial and distress – 'My grace is sufficient for thee: for my strength is made perfect in weakness. Most gladly therefore will I glory in my infirmities, that the power of Christ may rest upon me.'

This example of Paul's prayers for healing should not be used to argue against miraculous healing. Having confessed to his persisting 'thorn in the flesh', Paul went on immediately to remind the Christians at Corinth that: 'The signs of an apostle were performed among you with all endurance, by means both of signs and wonders and deeds of power' (2 Corinthians 12:12). Gordon Fee[1] points out that the phrase 'the signs of an apostle' only occurs here in the New Testament. He further suggests that Paul may distinguish between 'gifts of healing' and 'workings of miracles.' The important point remains that Paul 'sees no tension at all between the Spirit's activity in his ministry in this way and his own personal weaknesses about which he has been boasting.'

Post-Biblical Examples

In the same way as healing miracles are recorded as exceptional in the Bible, so it is with human life ever since. Whatever we make of the records of divine healing, all must surely acknowledge that

---

1. Fee, G. D., *God's Empowering Presence.* Paternoster Press, UK, 1995, p. 356.

during all these subsequent centuries everyone died. Sickness, disease and violence have pursued their relentless courses.

Claims have been made that various groups of Christians, living lives of moderation avoiding harmful excesses, experience less disease and longer lives than others. This may even include material prosperity resulting from something akin to the Puritan work ethic. The incidence of alcoholism, drug abuse and sexually transmitted diseases are surely lower amongst believing practising Christians than the general population. However, in the scale of population statistics, these differences will be marginal and overshadowed by the major influences of race, genetics and social factors such as poverty and deprivation.

In the general scheme of things Christians are not immune from sickness and suffering – in fact, their profession may incur suffering and even death. Many millions of Christians, of all races, ages and social groupings, down the centuries have lived, suffered and died. The experiences of a minute fraction of these have been recorded for us on account of their fame. But the vast majority remain unknown and unrecorded.

How then can we reconcile the sheer 'ordinariness' of the life experiences of most Christians, with the prediction Christ made to his disciples that those who believe on him would do his works. In fact, they would do 'greater works than these' (John 14:12). What are these greater works? The prediction is given added emphasis by his promising 'and whatsoever you shall ask in my name, that will I do; because I go unto my Father' (John 14:13).

11.

The Greater Works

'Verily, verily, I say unto you, He that believeth on me,
the works that I do shall he do also: and greater works
than these shall he do: because I go unto my Father.'
(John 14:12).

What did Jesus mean when he promised that his disciples would do greater works when he was no longer with them as a man on earth? What could be greater than raising the dead?

If we take this promise, coupled with the following one of having all our requests answered, we are left with a great dilemma. It simply has not happened and is not happening – that is, if we think of his promise on a purely physical level. The apparent non-fulfilment of the promise serves to show how superficial and materialistic our outlook can be. Do we really believe that when Jesus promised his disciples that if they spoke to a mountain and ordered it to move into the sea, they would see it happen? (Mark 11:23). It is not a lack of faith if we apply such a promise in a non-literal way.

Be happy and healthy

The human pursuit of happiness, including those who are Christians, is often, if not mainly, on the level of the enjoyment of health, wealth and the things that are pleasurable. These things are instinctively desirable to us. They are the things we seek and choose. Our lives are spent in cultivation of these things, in so far as we are able to do so.

When Jesus began his earthly ministry, he accepted these natural human desires. What we call his Sermon on the Mount, is predicated on these instincts. We are to pray for daily food. We should not give way to anxiety because God knows our needs. He will support us – therefore, relax and live a day at a time (Matthew 6:31-34). Having accepted these human needs, he goes on to underline his main message. What God looks for in a person's life is neither material nor physical.

In the Sermon on the Mount God's blessing rests on people who are experiencing, or who are, poor in spirit, mourning, meek, in a right relationship with God, merciful, pure in heart, peacemakers, persecuted for righteousness' sake, reviled by the world at large and slandered. This group of people is hardly one which is likely to attract many recruits. They are similar to those listed in Isaiah's prophecy as the type of persons whom the Messiah would reach and subsequently confirmed by Jesus as his natural constituency – the poor, the broken hearted, the captives, the blind, the imprisoned, the bruised (Isaiah 61: 1-3. Luke 4: 16-19). Imagine our political leaders giving out such a manifesto as an appeal for followers!

The message spelt out by Jesus should give the lie to any who would seek to enrol followers by promising health, wealth and prosperity. This is none other than a perversion of Jesus' stark depiction of his primary message.

The witness of the life of Jesus

We have no record of Jesus being ill. As far as the records we have, he had an uneventful life as a child and young man. He could enjoy, and enable others to enjoy, a marriage ceremony. He appreciated hospitality and the warmth of human relationships. He could use gentle humour and irony in his talk with people. But if there is one keynote or motif to his life it is in line with that prophesised that he would be 'a man of sorrows and acquainted with grief.' The entire fifty third chapter of Isaiah is a depiction of the coming Messiah who would be subjected to such suffering and sorrow that we would hide from it and him. Furthermore, this grief would be inflicted on him because of us and for us.

Reading this chapter in Isaiah and remembering the ways in which this was fulfilled in the life of Jesus and in all that led up to the Garden of Gethsemane and Calvary, we have an account of suffering that is unique in its intensity and nature. It was both physical and spiritual. In the middle of it, Jesus prayed a prayer that was not answered in one sense – that the experience should be avoided – whilst stating, at the same time, that he accepted his Father's will (Mark 14:32-42).

What should Christians expect?

The subsequent New Testament scriptures do not give us any justification for thinking that we will be spared suffering. They rather underline the call for identification with Christ in his suffering and even in his crucifixion, which will entail sacrifice and a cost. Paul was to put this graphically by declaring: *'I am crucified with Christ'* (Galatians 2:20). *'This is the way the master trod, and will not his servant still.'* What a contrast this provides with those smooth talkers conducting mass healing services in circumstances of opulence and personal aggrandisement.

Billy Graham wrote: 'Anyone who reads the Bible and comes away thinking that suffering is not to be the lot of the Christian is reading the Scriptures blindly and without understanding.'

Again I ask, how can we possibly hold out the claim or promise that the life of the Christian is one that is going to be one of 'roses all the way'?

What then are the 'greater works'?

As soon as Jesus made this prediction in John 14:12, that his disciples would do greater works, he went on to couple it with asking God in his name, 'that the Father may be glorified in the Son.' It was also coupled with the promise of the coming of a Comforter like Jesus. All this immediately preceded his own betrayal, trial and crucifixion.

In due time, following the ascension of Jesus Christ, this small band of disciples would be the channels for introducing a pagan world to the fact that this same Jesus was, and is, none other than the Son of God. He had come into the world to reconcile men and women to the God against whom they were rebelling. As they did this, dramatic miracles occurred to attest their stupendous claim. But the repeated challenge was the recognition that God had entered the world in the person of his Son, who had come to give himself that 'the world through him might be saved.' These were the people who would force their enemies to complain that they 'had turned the world upside down.' The offence caused by the early apostles and disciples was primarily for two reasons. Firstly, they preached Jesus Christ, crucified and resurrected as the only way to God. Secondly, their faith was heartfelt; to the extent that their chief critics had to acknowledge that 'they had been with Jesus' (Acts 4:13).

The evidence of the New Testament and subsequent history is that what began with Jesus Christ and a handful of followers rapidly became an ever increasing body of believers. In the first century after Christ there was an explosive growth in the number of those who believed in and followed Christ – far in excess of those who turned to Christ during his lifetime. All this happened without any great organisation, abundant financial resources or force of arms. Despite all the faults of organised Christianity, that growth has continued.

Whilst it is fair game to point to the defects in various branches of the professing Christian church, it would be a very blinkered critic who ignored the impact the Christian faith has made in the lives of countless of its followers and those touched by its beneficent mission in the world. Surely, the 'greater works', as compared with those seen from the carpenter's son from Nazareth, has been more than amply fulfilled over the last 2,000 years.

The greatness of the impact of Christ, through the agency of his followers, is also not to be measured on the basis of numbers, big events, let alone grand buildings or cathedrals. Jesus illustrated this so memorably when in Luke 15, he told the stories of the lost sheep, the lost coin and the lost son. The whole point of the three stories was the greatness and the wonder of a single person's reconciliation with God – *'likewise joy shall be in heaven over one sinner that repenteth, more than over ninety and nine just persons, which need no repentance'* (Luke 15:7).

James O. Fraser is a superb example of this claim. Here we have the case of a young man born into privileged circumstances – apart from the fact of the separation of his parents. Following public school and graduating in mathematics and engineering, he excelled as a pianist to potential concert standing. A promising career, or careers, lay ahead. Then he became convinced that God would have him serve in primitive inland China. The life Fraser lived amongst impoverished tribes entailed years of physical hardship, danger and privation. Added, or perhaps surpassing, all these tests was the apparent complete absence of any evidence of response to his endeavours. Fraser was certain that only prayer could change the situation amongst the Lisu people and other tribes – not only his prayers but also those of fellow Christians on the mission field and especially those thousands of miles away at home.

Fraser had illnesses, including intractable varicose ulceration and severe typhoid fever. He was to die from cerebral malaria at the age of 52 years. However, before his death he was to see amazing scenes of conversions and spiritual revival amongst the Lisu people and other tribes. He had no doubt that the dramatic change was in answer to faithful prayer. However, as one reads the accounts, including those recorded by his widow and one of his daughters, Eileen Crossman, there is little reference to his own physical and medical needs. We may be sure that in his final illness, intense prayer will have been made for his recovery, as surely will have been true in his previous illnesses. But there was no miraculous response. All we know is that there was an infinitely 'greater work.' In Fraser's own words: 'Can it be that a great work for God involving thousands of souls devolves upon our prayer life-half a world away?'[1]

---

1. Fraser, J. O. (Mrs.), *Fraser and Prayer.* Overseas Missionary Fellowship, London, 1963.

12.

Personal Experience

I have already referred several times to the way in which our backgrounds and beliefs precondition our responses to the question of miraculous healing. There is another even more personal dimension. This is our own experience of life as witnessed in our own lives as well as those of others. It is one thing to hold to certain theoretical or hypothetical positions. It is another how we come to terms with our own life experiences. This came home to me many years ago. I had attended a highly charged charismatic meeting in Bristol, when the speaker, who was staying with my wife and me, laid great emphasis on healing faith and how we needed to exercise it in obedience to the Holy Spirit. Immediately following the service, he approached me as to what could be done about some minor condition that was bothering him. I'm afraid I did not have the courage to tell him to take his own medicine.

I find it hard to listen to a young or middle aged preacher expound on coping with bereavement, when I know that he has had no experience of this within his own immediate family circle. Oswald Chambers comments on this in his book *The Shadow of an Agony*.[1] He rightly claims that: 'In a supreme agony something dies, no man is the same after it . . . and it is through a personal agony that a man is likely to begin to understand what the New Testament reveals. As long as we have our morality well within our own grasp, to talk about Jesus Christ and His Redemption is "much ado about nothing", but when a man's thick hide is pierced,

---

1. Chambers, O., *The Shadow of an Agony*. Marshall, Morgan & Scott, Edinburgh, 1934.

or he comes to his wits' end and enters the confines of an agony, he is apt to find that there is a great deal from which he has been shut away, and in his condition of suffering he discovers there is more in the Cross of Christ than intellectually he had thought possible . . . Circumstances are the things that twist a man's thinking into contortions.'

For these reasons I believe that anyone expressing his views should be prepared to reconcile these with his responses to events in his own life. Therefore, I give these personal and anecdotal memories.

I write this as I approach my 80th year. During these years I have been greatly blessed with good health. The only incidents worth recalling are acute appendicitis when a medical student (which it took me three days to diagnose, although the symptoms were typical of that which I had been taught!); Q fever caught in a laboratory in my thirties; acute pneumonia treated at home in my forties; an undiagnosed fulminating gastro-intestinal infection in my sixties, treated in a teaching hospital and moderate hypertension treated with drugs and which is symptomless. During all these I sought and followed medical advice. I also will have prayed – not for a miracle, but for healing and health.

Meanwhile, I thank God for good health. I do not wish to contract serious or fatal illness and fear pain. I do not wish to die. But I know that my times are in God's hands. Whatever this entails I do not know. But I am happy to leave this with Him – in fact, I do not believe I have any alternative! All I do know is that I am an eternal being and that when I die I shall be with Christ in a way too wonderful for me to imagine.

What about loved ones and friends?
This question poses, and has posed, more difficulties than those in respect of my own life.

My father died aged 77 years, having suffered nine months of painful illness caused by pancreatic cancer. He was a firm Christian believer to the end, but I am not aware of any impact on the course, or outcome, of his illness as a result of much prayer. My mother died at 93 years when age-associated degeneration had taken her mental faculties. My prayers in her case were essentially that the God in whom she had believed would take her to be with him.

These things came into sharp focus with my wife to whom I was married for 45 years. I had been on a winter sports holiday with my son and son-in-law. When I returned home Pam informed me that she would be going in to hospital within a few days for a biopsy. This resulted in a diagnosis of cancer of the uterus at the age of 55 years. The treatment took the form of a hysterectomy and bilateral removal of the ovaries. Within a few days the consultant pathologist phoned me where I was at work in my own hospital pathology department. He told me that Pam had a Mullerian tumour of the uterus. This took the form of a malignant combined carcinoma and sarcoma. These tumours are usually highly malignant. The pathologist sent me slides for me to see for myself. I then sent them to a nationally known gynaecological pathologist in the University of Manchester. She confirmed the diagnosis. The one bit of good news was that the tumour was in the form of a polyp, with no evidence of spread, so that it may have been removed completely. She said I would know within the following twelve months whether she had been cured or not. Further discussion took place with the local oncologists. In the end it was decided to 'play safe' and a course of radical radiotherapy was given.

My wife made an excellent recovery and enjoyed perfect health for the next fifteen years. During this time we often thanked God for her healing. The family and friends gathered for a memorable commemoration of her 70th birthday.

Within three months of her happy birthday Pam began to develop vague abdominal symptoms. She attended her general practitioner who referred her for an abdominal scan. I shall never forget going with her to the scanning department and the very long wait whilst I saw two of my radiologist colleagues go into the scanning room. Eventually, they emerged. They hardly needed to tell me that they had found tumours in her abdomen with free fluid collections. I drove Pam home, hardly being able to see the road ahead on account of tear-filled eyes. Then we sat around the kitchen table, trying to drink a cup of tea.

The next six months were taken up with further tests when a diagnosis of cancer of the pancreas with liver secondaries was made. During this time we prayed for a benign diagnosis. Then we prayed for a miracle. When I was away from home I would pray that when I returned I would find her feeling symptomatically improved. This did not happen. The disease was relentless in its course. Recurrent abdominal distension due to fluid collection, necessitated regular hospital admission for drainage.

Pam was admitted to the Macmillan Unit in my own hospital for symptom control for about three weeks. The oncologist, a personal friend and a Christian, met me. I had the message, although he did not articulate it precisely, that the end was approaching.

Pam and I decided that she would come home. Her pride and joy was the garden and I remember cutting the lawns and generally tidying up before collecting her from the hospital. She noticed. Then it was approximately six weeks at home, until I would spend the last night beside her bed, holding her hand until she took her last breath. It was such a strange feeling. It was as if one could see and hear her soul leave her body.

During these last months I prayed less and less for healing. I prayed more and more for her state of weakness and discomfort. Towards the end, my prayers were that God would take her to be with Him. That prayer was answered. As I type these words, my eyes are full of tears. There remains real grief over that time of parting. But there is also the sense of wonder that we are immortal souls. Pam was not a woman, my wife, who died from cancer. She was a person who had brought love and joy to her family and friends; who had experienced God's love in Christ and had gone to be with Him.

Pam's verse, which she clung to during her final weeks, was from Nahum 1:7 – *'The Lord is good, a stronghold in the day of trouble; and he knoweth them that trust in him.'* The verse which I had inscribed on her tombstone, is Philippians 1:21 – *'For me to live is Christ, and to die is gain.'* In Pam's case these words are not convenient quotes. They express perfectly her faith and experience. They are true.

Personal Reflections
I hope that the above record is not intrusive or an embarrassment to any reader. However, I believe it is necessary in any discussion of this topic to be consistent with one's own experience and practice. As I reflect on this I have to confess that when I prayed for healing during Pam's first encounter with cancer, I believed that God had answered my prayers and those of other Christians. However, I cannot point to a miracle of healing. The diagnosis followed a course which was in line with conventional medical practice.

I have one caveat and lingering regret. Did we lack the faith to reject the offer of radical radiotherapy during the first appearance of cancer? Was the radiotherapy the cause of the development of further malignancy fifteen years later?

When it came to the final illness, did I really believe that God would heal her? I honestly do not know the answer. As I think back on those months, I become more convinced that Pam herself accepted the diagnosis, came to terms with it and realised the cancer would pursue its natural course in the same way as she had witnessed it repeatedly as she cared for terminally ill cancer sufferers in the course of her medical work in Palliative Care.

My own failure was in seeking every avenue, including the spiritual one, to 'fight' the disease. This meant that we did not talk together as frankly as Pam might have desired. Early in her final illness she would broach the subject of my life after she had died. But I could not pursue it and face the reality of the inevitable. In this respect I still feel guilty that perhaps she was unable to unburden as she might have wished. Such are some of the 'agonies' to which Oswald Chambers referred to above. They certainly put into perspective glib and superficial claims to miraculous healing as a right or as part of the atonement of Christ.

Oswald Chambers' book is based on a series of talks he gave to soldiers in YMCA camps and huts in Egypt during the 1914-18 world war. Chambers was to die in Egypt in 1917 at the age of 43 years. At a time of catastrophe and world-wide upheaval in the lives of so many, Chambers seems to have been given remarkable insight, which is as relevant today as when he taught and wrote – if not more so. 'There is not civilised security anywhere on the globe. We have seen there is no such thing as a Christian nation, and we have seen the unutterable futility of the organised Christian Church.' He underlined that the basic feature of human life is tragic and that the way out made by God in Redemption is approached through suffering.

13

What shall we then say?

The effort to be fair or balanced often results in uncertainty or confusion. I set out with an apparently simple question – does God do miracles of healing in response to prayer and faith? There are some responses which I would expect all, or most, to accept.

1. The course of illness or disease in one person is unpredictable – sometimes to a remarkable degree.
2. Rarely, what may be accepted as an inevitably rapidly fatal disease, may go into remission and disappear completely, in the absence of medical treatment or any claim to divine or 'spiritual' healing.
3. Many claims for miraculous healing do not stand up to scrutiny or impartial investigation. This applies to claims made on a Christian basis as well as non-Christian ones.

If the above are accepted, thereafter some radically divergent attitudes begin to emerge. In the case of the agnostic or atheist, there is no problem. If cases of dramatic or miraculous healing are presented, they simply appear to be such because of our ignorance of a rational explanation. If only we knew the chemical, physiological or psychological etc. mechanism, we should be able to explain the event.

Christians will respond in a variety of ways, depending on their faith bases. I have many Christian friends whom, in some ways, I envy for their simple unquestioning faith. They recognise that God has healed from the time of man's creation. Jesus and his disciples performed miracles of healing. Therefore, we should expect the same today. I talk to believing friends who say they have seen the lame walk; crutches and wheelchairs discarded; cancers disappear and actually observed a leg in the process of its miraculous lengthening. In the case of the latter, and despite the stiffness associated with my own advancing years, I could lie on my back and make one heel extend beyond the other without giving visible evidence of the tilt of my pelvis! The point is that such a demonstration would, I am sure, not disabuse my Christian friend of the validity of his claim to have witnessed such a miracle.

Sometimes, during discussions on divine, miraculous healing, or when facing disease personally or in others, the comment is made 'Yes, I believe that God can do anything. I believe that God can intervene and heal.' What Christian can possibly deny such a bald statement? But does it follow that God *will* heal in a given situation? Furthermore, should we expect God to act against all natural law? If we should think, for example, of a man who is an above-knee amputee – in such a case, is it legitimate that prayer should be made for restoration in the form of a normal leg? Surely, many Christians would say that such prayer would be misplaced if not silly. In this example, it is no answer to say that 'God can do anything.' This rather reflects on the nature of a 'God' of a person's imagination. It is akin to the quoted examples of claims of lost dental fillings being replaced by new ones – especially when they are of gold and of a cruciform outline!

During my years as a consultant pathologist I performed several hundreds of post-mortem examinations on coalminers from the valleys of South Wales. Many of these had coal workers' pneumoconiosis. In its severe form of what was termed PMF ('progressive massive fibrosis'), the normal spongy lung tissue had been replaced by large, black, solid lumps. These areas could be partly calcified and could only be cut or sawn through with difficulty. These lumps could be so large as to have replaced more than 80% of normal lung. There could be no natural cure or remission of this condition. The only change would be when a ragged cavity might form, usually as a result of superimposed tuberculous infection. This was obviously not a cure but an aggravation of the condition that presaged death.

In the case of these coalminers, some of them were Christians known personally to me in contacts at churches, chapels and mission halls. They were devout men who lived lives of undeviating faith in the God who had revealed himself to them in Jesus Christ. They believed their Bibles. They lived prayerful lives, bringing their daily affairs, and any major concerns, to God in simple faith. They would pray about their lung disability, shortness of breath and intercurrent infections. However, I do not know of any that prayed for a cure for their pneumoconiosis graded as 100% severity. Furthermore, if I knew of one of this nature, I would have in my mind's eye a picture of the state of that man's lungs as I have described above. The 'cure' of such a lung would entail a miracle as dramatic as that of a restoration of a limb to an amputee. In the face of human disease of this order, is it really honest to retreat to a position that cannot be refuted by clinging to the claim 'I believe that God can do anything'?

I cannot comply with a simple acceptance of a general ministry of miraculous healing of physical disease in our generation. My response, based on many years of reflection, practice as a doctor and pathologist, study of the evidence as afforded both by those making healing claims as well as those debunking them, and finally by grappling with biblical history, is that a simplistic acceptance of contemporary miraculous healing, is not credible. This reserve is then confirmed in the lives and deaths of Christians – both well-known and generally unknown.

Having taken such a reserved position, I am then challenged because I see no clear scriptural grounds for the cessationist argument that God limited miraculous divine healing to New

Testament times. In fact, this claim carries with it great danger. The question then arises – what other gifts, divine intervention or activity should be similarly limited? It also may undermine our understanding of, and belief in, the meaning and power of prayer. Why pray if God has stopped working on that level? I find that books which claim that the gift of healing ceased in the post-apostolic age are usually silent on this danger and the implications of their position.

I suggest there are at least three ways in which the gullibility of an over – ready acceptance of claims of miraculous healing can be reconciled with an over-strict rejection of this dimension of divine activity in our day.

1. The first is an acceptance that God does still heal miraculously, but that this is now highly exceptional. It happens when there is a near unique set of circumstances and need – and especially as a *sign* – for example, as claimed by Jean-Pierre Bely at Lourdes and narrated in chapter 8. We may debate the degree of rarity of such instances. We do not know, but I believe this to be exceedingly rare nowadays. It is certainly not replicated *en masse* at man's behest in crowded meetings for healing, other than when there is a turning to God for salvation in the broader sense – see below.

2. Secondly, we must re-affirm that **all** healing is an integral part of divine activity, by the God of creation and purpose. Any knowledge of the complexity and intricate inter-relationships that work to keep us alive causes us to marvel, not that we sometimes sicken and die, but that we live so effortlessly for most of the time. All the mechanisms are there for growth, repair, replacement, homeostasis (the correction of extremes that ensures stability) and haemostasis (blood clotting).

3. Having accepted that healing is God's gift, the Christian of whatever persuasion, should have no problem in

acknowledging and rejoicing that God's greatest healing activity is spiritual. There is a vogue for 'holistic medicine' and treating the 'whole person.' The Christian must maintain that only the God and Father of the Lord Jesus Christ can truly exercise this form of healing. The biblical teaching on salvation, wholeness, health and righteousness, repeatedly stresses this message, both in doctrine and by example. This, in fact, is the grand theme of the Bible, where the physical dimension is merely incidental or illustrative. Sin is the principal impediment to wholeness, so that the man 'made whole' is told to 'sin no more.' (John 5:14).

The third argument, stressing the dimension of spiritual healing is one that may justify some of the claims for the happenings at Lourdes or other meetings. I cannot share the emphasis that may be placed on Mary, the saints and relics, but it does not then follow that the Holy Spirit may not work bringing conviction of sin, acceptance of Jesus Christ and reconciliation with God. In fact, this is the stress in some of the testimonies. It also emphasises the need to recognise that the healing of salvation is usually something that happens within the fellowship of Christ's true church.

The suffering Christ and the suffering church

Whenever we may rejoice in healing, whether in the physical or spiritual dimension, we should stop to remember the cost of our salvation. Some have rendered the description of the 'blessed' saying of Jesus in Matthew 5, as his 'happiness sayings.' This I believe is seriously misleading. After all, the categories of people to which Jesus applies this description are generally in states we would naturally avoid – the poor, the broken-hearted, the mourning and the reviled. The birth, life and death of Jesus Christ entailed uniquely intense suffering. Those who have followed Him have, in some degree shared in his suffering – some to the point of laying down their lives. This still obtains in today's world.

In the light of this, how then can any Christian claim that physical relief and healing, as a result of our requests, are an integral part of the atonement purchased by Christ on Calvary – just waiting for us to claim it?

Surely, we as Christians, who may for this time, be spared such identification with Christ's suffering, rather humble ourselves, praying that if or when such should be our lot we may, by God's grace, be able to know something of the joy which they show as they count it a privilege to share in Christ's suffering. Here we enter the heart of the mystery of the Christian gospel. We can live our lives on such a theoretical level, with glib assertions of our relationship to God. But what of times of testing? John Stam, a missionary in China in the 1930's, was greatly impressed by a poem entitled 'Afraid', written by a Presbyterian missionary E. H. Hamilton.[1] This was written following the martyrdom of J. W. Vinson in northern China. Prior to his execution by rebel Chinese soldiers, they menaced him, waving a gun before him, asking: 'Are you afraid?' He replied: 'No, if you shoot, I go straight to heaven.' Later his decapitated body was found.

> *Afraid? Of What?*
> *To feel the spirit's glad release/*
> *To pass from pain to perfect peace,*
> *The strife and strain of life to cease?*
> *Afraid – of that?*

> *Afraid? Of What?*
> *Afraid to see the Savior's face,*
> *To hear His welcome, and to trace*
> *The glory gleam from wounds of grace?*
> *Afraid – of that?*

---

1. Christie, V., *John and Betty Stam*. Christian Focus Publications, Scotland, 2008.

Afraid? Of What?
A flash, a crash, a pierced heart;
Darkness, light, O Heaven's art!
A wound of His a counterpart!
Afraid? – of that?

Afraid? Of What?
To do by death what life could not –
Baptize with blood a stony plot,
Till souls shall blossom from the spot?
Afraid? – of that?

On the 8th December 1934, John Stam and his wife Betty, were themselves to pay with their lives, in a barbaric scene, for their identification with Christ in His suffering. They left a precious baby girl of three months.[2]

---

2. White, K., *John and Betty Stam*. Minneapolis: Bethany, 1989.

14.

The Final Chapter – or is it?

'The last enemy that shall be destroyed is death.'
(1 Corinthians 15:26).

'Death is nothing to us. For what has been dissolved has no sense-experience, and what has no sense-experience is nothing to us.'
(Epicurus).

'The nature of 'physical' death is highly negotiable; in recent times Western tests have shifted from cessation of spontaneous breathing to 'brain death'. This involves more than the matter of a truer definition; it corresponds with western values (which prize the brain) and squares with the capacities of hospital technology. Some cultures think of death as a sudden happening, others regard dying as a process advancing from the moment of birth and continuing beyond the grave. Bodies are thus languages as well as envelopes of the flesh.'
(R. Porter).[1]

The above contrasts the clarity of the Christian position in the face of death with that of the bewilderment and ambiguity of the alternatives.

Man's uniqueness is seen in the early development of an advanced degree of self-awareness. This makes him unique in having self-knowledge that his life is limited and that he faces

---

1. Porter, R., *The greatest benefit to mankind.* Harper Collins, London, 1997.

death. For the majority of people, under 'ordinary' circumstances this is something that disturbs us, or, at least, we prefer not to dwell on the subject.

Life-threatening illness and disease disturb us for at least two reasons:

1. The problem of pain and suffering.
2. The fear of death.

Coping with pain

'God whispers to us in our pleasures, speaks to us in our conscience, but shouts in our pains: it is His megaphone to rouse a deaf world.'
(C. S. Lewis).[2]

The problem of pain remains a problem, no matter how often it is considered, debated and written about. C. S. Lewis treats it as such. The great grief of his latter years came after he had already heard God's voice. I also doubt whether he would regard pain as God's infliction – at least in the majority of instances.

I have already referred to Paul Brand's work on the purpose and valuable function of pain sensation. But, as Brand himself recognised, there is so much pain that seems gratuitous without any obvious purpose. We also must recognise the entire gamut of symptoms which may accompany disease that may almost destroy a person. Nausea, vomiting and shortness of breath come into this category. A feature that is often unrecognised is that of overwhelming weakness and fatigue. This may not be articulated clearly even when the patient is receiving the best of modern palliative care.

Christians are not immune from these aspects of suffering. John Wesley's claim that 'our people die well' may express a truth in that a Christian should be at peace in his or her relationship with God and others, as well as having an assurance of a future

2. Lewis, C. S., *The Problem of Pain.* MacMillan Co., New York, 1955, p. 83.

with God in heaven. However, this is by no means always the case. I have witnessed terminal illness in Christians who have lived lives of faithful and joyful service, who were strong in faith and able to strengthen others. Yet, as they faced their own death they were plunged into deep anxiety, showing signs of depression that was in complete contrast to their normal character.

The problem in such situations may well be a straightforward medical one. The provision of adequate pain relief and addressing symptomatic needs is an over-riding requirement. Prayer and spiritual consolation, as well as the presence of a true sympathiser, may well diminish the intensity of suffering, but these should not be used as substitutes for the provision of any medical means that could be helpful.

Dr James Casson, writing his booklet on 'Dying' as he faced his own death from cancer at the age of 37 years deals with this aspect with the honesty of first-hand experience:[3] *'As one grows weaker, shorter of breath, distended and uncomfortable, so living becomes more and more of an effort. It is hard not to grow selfish when the simplest matters become like a preparation for a twenty mile hill walk. Emotions are squeezed out like an empty tooth-paste tube. There are no reserves left. Against this background all but the greatest saints will become moody and irritable, making unkind or hurtful remarks to those they love most.'*

'Death Undefeated' – this is the title of a leading article written by Ivan Illich in the *British Medical Journal*.[4] Illich writes from the standpoint of an agnostic, but his analysis is, in my view, a brilliant one which has relevance to all, whether a Christian believer or otherwise. He says you can prepare to die as a Stoic, an Epicurean or as a Christian. I have already referred to his critique that our lives and health have been medicalised. He maintains that the same has happened in respect of death. *'The end of life can only be postponed. And for many, this managed*

3. Casson, J., *Dying, The Greatest Adventure of my Life.* Christian Medical Fellowship, London, 1980.
4. Illich, I., 'Death Undefeated', *BMJ*, 1995, 311:1652-3.

postponement has been lifelong; at death it is an uninterrupted memory.' Whereas, as in previous times, many people's most intense involvement with medicine occurred as they approached death, nowadays this extends through our lives to our final illness. This has made *'the task of family, friends, or chaplain: to arouse the dying person's willingness to accept the inevitable, to find strength in the beauty of memories, and to take leave of the world, all the more difficult.'* He, indirectly, blames medicine for usurping the role that used to be exercised by Christianity *'I analysed the medical enterprise as a post-Christian liturgy that instilled a keen fear of pain, disability, and death in its devotees.'*

When I re-read Illich's article I am ever more struck by his insight, which is even more relevant today than when he wrote 15 years ago, to both Christian and non-Christian. I appreciate that I am not addressing this subject in relation to those of a non-Christian religion. This is not my theme, but I believe that if this were to be analysed, other religions would fit into Illich's groups of Stoic or Epicurean philosophies as far as attitudes to death and the hereafter. It is noteworthy that philosophers have faced the challenge of death when many Christians have maintained a discrete silence. Socrates in his *Phaedo* said that: 'True philosophers make dying their profession.' The stoic Seneca claimed: 'He will live badly who does not know how to die well.'

The fear of death
There are many in the world whose lives are so miserable, so painful and hopeless, that death may not appear as a dreaded intruder – it may even be welcomed. But for most of us, leading 'normal' lives, the thought of our own death is something we try to avoid. As we age we remember that 'time is running out.' But at such times death can appear even more objectionable.

All people subscribe to one of two belief systems:

1. Mankind is mortal and there is no life after death.
2. Mankind is immortal and there is life after death.

Socrates summarised these alternatives after death 'Either it is annihilation, and the dead have no consciousness of anything; or, as we are told, it is really a change: a migration of the soul from this place to another.' He personalised the choice when he was condemned to death, telling his accusers and the jury – 'Now is the time that we were going, I to die and you to live; but which of us has the happier prospect is unknown to anyone but God.'

Todd May, in his book *Death*,[5] makes it clear that he is writing as an atheist and does not believe in an after-life. He affirms that: 'The fact that we die is the most important fact about us. There is nothing that has more weight in our lives.' He acknowledges that: 'consciousness itself is much more than merely being aware. It is also being involved. And the prospect of losing those involvements is a central part of the pain of knowing one is mortal.' However, being alive is more than experiences, good or bad, or involvement. May then quotes Thomas Nagel – 'There are elements which, if added to one's experience, make life better; there are other elements which, if added to one's experience make life worse. But what remains when these are set aside is not merely neutral: it is emphatically positive . . . The additional positive weight is supplied by experience itself, rather than by any of its contents.' In other words, life itself is precious. Just being alive is more than an expression of chemistry and physiology.

In view of the above, the concept of immortality gives May a great problem, but he approaches it with admirable honesty. This is partly because he postulates that an indefinite and interminable existence would be a daunting prospect. In fact, immortality would itself be an evil just as death is. It would be a fate worse than death! 'Many of the virtues we associate with human life would go missing if we were immortal. Courage, for instance, would be absent,since it would be impossible to risk one's life for anything . . . personal relationships would become less serious . . . bonds between parents and children would slacken.' The reality

---

5. Todd, May, *Death*. Acumen, Stocksfield, 2009.

of death and its appreciation gives life a shape, urgency and beauty. 'Mortality is not an evil. It is all a question of timing. One must live long enough that one's passion for living remains intact. Less than that and one dies bored with life.' This raises the question, is there a good time to die? It also challenges the Christian understanding of the nature and quality of immortality and eternal life.

The majority view in the developed world would appear to be that life ends in death. At the most, if anything lasts, it is in the genes and memories of our children, friends and in the structures and ethos of our communities. For those with exceptional talents, they will leave a legacy of cultural activities. These legacies could be for ill as well as good!

Evidently, such belief systems are compatible with loving human relationships, caring communities and those things which contribute to the enrichment of humanity. Having acknowledged these aspects, if this life is all there is, how can we avoid a state of inevitable pessimism? There is for the person no hope, no future and nothing better. Every aspect of life, and especially the happy ones, are overshadowed – '*every joy is touched with pain. Shadows fall on brightest hours.*' We fear that each temporary parting from a loved one, may prove to be the last one.

It is common for gospel preachers to use quotations from near death bed scenes of atheists to contrast their hopelessness with that of the death of the Christian who is resting and trusting in his relationship with Jesus Christ. I admit that this may be an unfair over-simplification, but yet it is still a valid contrast.

Billy Graham, in his book *Armageddon*[6] quotes the dying words attributed to Christians –

John Knox – 'Live in Christ, die in Christ and the flesh need not fear death.'

6. Graham, B., *Till Armageddon. A Perspective on Suffering.* Hodder and Stoughton, London, 1981, p. 202.

The Final Chapter – or is it?

John Wesley – 'The best of all is, God is with us.'

Richard Baxter – 'I have pain – but I have peace.'

Graham's own grandmother – 'I see Jesus, and He has His hand outstretched to me. And there is Ben, and he has both his eyes and both of his legs.' Ben was Graham's grandfather had lost an eye and a leg at Gettysburg.

Graham contrasts these with Voltaire's cry – 'I am abandoned by God and man! I shall go to hell! O Christ, O Jesus Christ!' Here I must interject that accounts of Voltaire's last words when he died at the age of 84 years are various and contradictory – see Critchley (2009).

When I worked for a general practitioner in Ayrshire, shortly after qualifying, he gave me a piece of paper on which he had written words which he said had been given to him by James Bridie, the pseudonym of Osborne Henry Mavor, the Scottish doctor and dramatist. Mavor became a consulting physician and professor, but gave it up to write plays. He returned to medicine in the second world war, during which he lost a son. I suspect the following was written following this experience shortly before his own death in 1951.

> '*I must awa', awa', awa',*
> *There's naethin here at a', at a', at a';*
> *I kenna whaur I'm gaun, I'm gaun, I'm gaun,*
> *I'm jes heing pitten on, pitten on, pitten on;*
> *It may he fear or faur, or faur, or faur,*
> *But it canna be nae waur, nae waur, nae waur.*'

Having quoted the above from Christians and non-Christians, I would add that history and personal experience serve to show this pattern is not invariable. Therefore, I am anxious that I should not fall into the trap of quoting Christians who go out in a blaze of glory affirming their faith, whilst unbelievers bemoan their fate in cries of desperation.

Adam Smith,[7] commenting on the death of his friend, David Hume in 1776, said that he departed: 'with great cheerfulness and good humour and with more real resignation to the necessary course of things than any whining Christian ever died with pretended resignation to the will of God' – what a rebuke to glib claims on our part as professing Christians.

This is in keeping with David Hume's own words in his *My Own Life*, written in 1775, when he knew he had developed his final illness –

'I now reckon upon a speedy dissolution. I have suffered very little pain from my disorder; and what is more strange, have, notwithstanding the great decline of my person, never suffered a moment's abatement of spirits; insomuch that were I to name a period of my life which I should most choose to pass over again, I might be tempted to point to this later period. I possess the same ardour as ever in study and the same gaiety in company; I consider, besides, that a man of sixty-five, by dying, cuts off only a few years of infirmities; and though I see many symptoms of my literary reputation's breaking out at last with additional lustre, I know that I could have but few years to enjoy it. It is difficult to be more detached from life than I am at present.'

These words of David Hume and more that followed, I accept as a challenge to the danger of glibness that sometimes characterises accounts of death-bed triumphalism on the part of Christians. None of us know what our last words will be, let alone our last thought.

It is not easy, when reading Dr Axel Munthe's book,[8] to determine how much is factual autobiography from what is

---

7. Huxley, *Hume*. MacMillan and Co., 1869, p. 42.
8. Munthe, A., *The Story of San Michele*. John Murray, London, 1929.

embellishment. Leaving this question aside, there are two moving accounts of dying and death towards the end of his book. The first was the death of his faithful retainer Pacciale. Munthe remembered him as 'the most honest, the most clean-minded, the most guileless man I have ever met in any land and in any station of life, gentle as a child.' Pacciale had a simple, devout, catholic faith. One day he simply said he felt tired. Then he went to lie down – something he had never done previously throughout his hard life. When Munthe entered the room during the evening he found the household and friends sitting around the room. The priest came with the last sacrament. Old Pacciale gave his confession and asked forgiveness. He nodded his head and kissed the crucifix and peacefully passed into eternity.

Munthe goes on to describe the sadness of his own last days. He engages in a reverie which reminds him of the delights which he will no longer experience. In particular he has had to leave his beloved San Michele. He asks himself: 'Why should I think about death? God in his mercy has made Death invisible to the eyes of man . . . Strangest of all, the further we advance towards our graves, the further does Death recede from our thoughts. Indeed it needed a God to perform such a miracle! Old people seldom talk about death, their dim eyes seem unwilling to focus anything but the past and the present.' Munthe sees his life as a battle over and lost. He has accepted his fate. As he lapses into a dream-like reverie he sees himself at the gate of heaven, confronting St. Peter. The interchanges at the gate are rather like a humanistic version of Bunyan's pilgrim's triumphant entry. This, to me, is the tragedy of his vision – namely the lack of any assurance. In its place there is the vague, ill-defined plea that he will appease the Grand Inquisitor largely on account of his love of and care for animals.

Dr Theodore Dalrymple, whilst reviewing Emile Zola's collection of short stories, *How We Die*, emphasises how we are so concerned with our own affairs, that we crowd out the reality of our own. 'I used to watch mourners at funerals from my study window overlooking a splendid church, Most of the mourners – the men, anyway, furtively looked at their watches, consulted their diaries, or sent text messages, as if funerals were primitive ceremonies conducted by a strange tribe (the dead) of no possible application to them.'[9]

Simon Critchley has written a book *The Book of Dead Philosophers*.[10] This provides a fascinating record, not only of the dying attitudes and affirmations of famous philosophers, but also snapshots of their lives. He states his purpose as: 'I want to defend the ideal of the philosophical death. In a world where the only metaphysics in which people believe is either money or medical society and where longevity is prized as an unquestioned good, I do not deny that this is a difficult ideal to defend. Yet, it is my belief that philosophy can teach a readiness for death without which any conception of contentment, let alone happiness, is illusory.' The difficulty is that reading this interesting, even highly entertaining book, is that so many philosopher's deaths have been dismal affairs, whilst their lives leading up to the final scene have been unmitigated disaster areas.

Critchley himself writes taking an Epicurean stance – although he takes pains to distance himself from the parody of contemporary Epicureanism with its eat, drink and be merry type of life. He takes the true teaching to be one of prudence in all matters. Given this personal attitude I am impressed with Critchley's insight into the Christian position. He examines the teaching and examples of early Christians from the time of Paul and concludes: 'It is important, I think, in cultures like our own where Christianity has become so trivialised, to remind oneself of this considerably more rigorous and demanding Christian attitude towards death.'

Perhaps we should do well to leave this aspect of dying with the account of the contrast of the two men crucified on either side of Jesus – the one reviling to the end and the other praying in simple trust that Jesus would receive him after death.

---

9. Dalrymple, T., 'The Spur of Death', *BMJ*, 2010:340:340-c2491.
10. Critchley, S., *The Book of Dead Philosophers*. Granta Publications, London. 2009.

The Christian facing death

Courage is a human quality and I have already recognised that Christians have no monopoly of this. Christian hope, however, is a gift. It is something that is received by faith. It is based on God and the reliability of his word of promise.

C. S. Lewis was 'surprised by joy.' This joy is independent of circumstances and may exist in defiance of them. Every believer must have had the experience of seeing a major tragedy in the life of a Christian friend or relative, who by nature, had shown a tendency to be upset by trivia, and therefore feared how he or she would cope – only to witness a genuine serenity and acceptance despite all that had happened. This can only be understood by the one certainty in the Christian's life.

> *'Christ alone has life in Himself, and we have it by His gift by union with Him either here or hereafter. It makes a vast difference between the philosophic and the religious treatment of immortality when we remember this – that in the Bible the supreme interest and final ground of immortality was not the continuity of an organism, physical or psychical, but of a relation. The ground of belief was not that such an organism must go on, but that a life in God, and especially the risen Christ could not die'* (P. T. Forsyth).[11]

In commenting of 2 Timothy 1:10, '. . . *our Saviour Jesus Christ, who hath abolished death, and hath brought life and immortality to light through the gospel'*, John Stott writes, *'One of the most searching tests to apply to any religion concerns its attitude to death. And measured by this test much so-called Christianity is found wanting, with its black clothes, its mournful chants and its requiem masses. Of course, dying can be unpleasant, and bereavement can bring bitter sorrow. But death itself has been overthrown, and 'blessed are the dead who die in the Lord' (Revelation 14:13). The proper*

---

11. Forsyth, P. T., *This Life and the Next*. Independent Press, 1953. (First published in 1918.)

epitaph to write for a Christian believer is not a dismal and uncertain petition RIP (rest in peace) but a joyful and certain affirmation CAD (Christ hath abolished death), or – if you prefer the classical languages – its Greek or Latin equivalent.'[12]

These are not theoretical comments by theologians. They provide the basis for a confidence that has been displayed by countless believers, both of famous people as well as those not known to the public.

Mozart, who died at the age of 35, wrote this letter to his father on the 4th April 1787:

> '*Since death (to be precise) is the true end and purpose of life, I have made it my business over the past few years to get to know this true, this best friend of man so well that the thought of him, not only knows no terrors for me, but even brings me great comfort. I thank God has granted me the good fortune and opportunity to get to know death as the key to our true happiness.*
>
> *I never go to bed without reflecting on the thought that perhaps, young as I am, the next day I might not be alive any more. And no man who knows me will be able to say that in social intercourse I am morose or sad. For this happiness I thank every day my Creator, and with all my heart I wish this happiness for all my fellow-men.'*

There was more to Mozart than music alone!

In a more modern testimony, Terence Molyneux wrote movingly in the *British Medical Journal* of 26th July 1980, of how, when aged 43 years, he was walking along a corridor when the sound of his footsteps altered unmistakably. Then he found his legs were weak. There followed a series of medical consultations until a diagnosis of motor neurone disease was made. He was given a

---

12. Stott, J. R. W., *Guard the Gospel. The Message of 2 Timothy Today.* IVP, London, 1973, p. 39.

life-expectancy of four years in 1975. By 1978 walking was no longer possible. A converted automatic Allegro car kept him on the road until December 1978 when his hands began to fail. This put an end to his skills in typing, piano, oboe and saxophone playing. At the time of writing he was completely crippled, and began his account by recalling that on the very day when he first became aware of his disease, an 'astonishing peace' entered his life. Now he could say: *'Days speed by; life is intensely, albeit quietly, full; but when dying is forecast (correctly or not) for a rather proximate future, description is really beggared. An extract from the sacred writings of the Christian faith has precisely what I want to say under this head . . . "Who shall separate us from the love of Christ?" And to the list of tribulation, distress, persecution, famine, nakedness, peril, sword, death, life, angels, principalities, powers, things present, things to come, height, depth, or any other creature.'* Molyneux affirms: *'To that list I add "nor motor neurone disease" and with his conclusion I gladly concur – none of these shall be able to separate us from the love of God which is in Christ Jesus our Lord'* (Romans 8:38, 39).

Dr James Casson, to whom I have already referred was candid in his admission of periods of bitterness against God – that is, until: *'Peace of mind came suddenly when reading "Daily light" one evening in February – "in all their affliction he was afflicted" (Isaiah 63:9). The New Testament teaching on suffering takes us into an entirely different sphere. Our Lord is not standing by seeing how we get on, he is actually suffering with us. Our pain is his pain, our swollen useless limbs are his, but ultimately our weakness becomes his strength and our defeat becomes his victory . . . Assurance is something all true believers should know as they approach death, a deep peace of mind. The Bible speaks of this as "the anchor of the soul". Whatever physical buffeting we may experience, and even should we capsize, our ship is unsinkable and this anchor will always hold. While the sense of bereavement is never inappropriate or to be looked back on with regrets, clearer Bible teaching is desperately needed in our churches today.'*

I have quoted the above examples at some length, because I believe it is singularly inappropriate for healthy, untroubled people to prescribe how anyone approaching death should think or behave, whether they be Christians or not. We may and should try to understand the biblical teaching on the subject, but it then remains a subject. Having done that, all we can do is to observe examples such as these quoted and pray that God will graciously grant us to trust in him in a similar way when our time comes. This will also protect us against some of the glib excesses of those who would major on the possibility of dramatic, miraculous intervention, when the time has come to face the reality of dying and death.

In 1966, I heard the Rev. Raymond Lawrence, then of Weston-super-Mare, speak of an experience he had when he was a minister in London. He was designated to speak at a civic service in central London. He preached the Christian gospel message. As he shook hands with the departing congregation and extended his hand to one man, it was literally knocked away. This man was the chairman of the Water Board and of many other important committees. Three weeks later this man's wife phoned Lawrence to say that her husband wished to see him. His doctors had diagnosed disseminated cancer. During the interim he had been born again as a Christian and his remaining days were characterised by an extraordinary growth in grace and knowledge of the Bible. Just before his death he told Lawrence that he must conduct his funeral service. He said: 'You will doubtless observe the usual conventions in referring to my civic life, etc., but cut it short and tell them more about the man they never knew – the man of the last week.' Lawrence did this and many were moved.

What of the medical care of the Christian in presumed terminal illness?

In days of increased and increasing medicalisation of illness and death, should medical care be tailored to the beliefs or views of the patient? The fact that the question can be posed is itself significant. Patient autonomy has become a buzz-word in medical ethics. Any hint of paternalism on the part of the doctor is deemed highly regrettable. The ironic aspect of this is that it is often precisely in the approach to lethal illness or dying that patients may be in the greatest danger of losing their autonomy – and all this at the time when the pressure for assisted suicide is increasing steadily.

End-of-life decisions are not the subject under discussion, but I raise it at this point simply to point out that the seriously ill or dying person is peculiarly at risk from the attitudes of others, both of friends, family and medical staff. Just as doctors may be guilty of attempts to prolong life unnaturally, so may misguided 'miracle workers' try to use the label of the Christian faith to engender hope in hopeless situations.

The possible conflict between the medical attendant's lack of faith and the patient's Christian faith is illustrated in a case described by Ohnsorge and Ford.[13] They describe the case of a 70-year-old man who had end-stage chronic obstructive pulmonary disease. He was semi-dependant on mechanical ventilation. The patient developed life-threatening bowel obstruction on top of all his troubles. The patient refused surgical intervention. He also refused to have a DNR (do not resuscitate) notice. The patient gave his reason saying that he was a Christian so that 'Only God knows when it is my time.' He felt ready to accept death. As a result of this an 'ethics consultation service' meeting was held. This comprised the patient, physician, a full-time ethicist and a visiting bioethics doctoral candidate – this was in the USA! When the patient mentioned prayer and God several times, the authors describe the family noting the 'eye-rolling' reaction of the physician. There was clearly concern that this patient's expressed faith in God could be an indication of mental disturbance which affected his ability to decide for himself. The story has a delightful

13. Ohnsorge, K. and Ford, P. J., in *Complex Ethics Consultations. Cases that haunt us.* Edited by P. J. Ford and D. M. Dudzinski. Cambridge University Press, 2008, p. 155.

ironic ending. 'He continued to express his faith that God would direct his course of treatment. When we returned the second day the patient was alert and smiling. He told us that the physicians believed his bowel problem had resolved . . . the patient was now eating solid food and was not vomiting. The patient was discharged to home the following day without a DNR order . . . Had his faith saved him? Or, did the pervasive uncertainty endemic to medical prognostication create a false picture? How could we tell the difference? . . . These questions certainly come to mind as we face other patients with beliefs different from our own.' These authors are to be admired for their honesty. My worry arises when such honesty and humility are lacking on the part of those who have care of the sick. This applies both to those exercising direct medical intervention, but also to those who may play a critical role as next of kin or friends.

15.

The Resting Place

'Almighty God is the Lord of life and death, and of all things to them pertaining, as youth, strength, health, age, weakness and sickness.'
(Book of Common Prayer
– The Visitation of the Sick).

In a variety of bible studies and discussion groups, as well as in private conversations, I have been asked: 'Do you believe in healing miracles?' This is a question I decline to answer. The question is ill-defined and not capable of a soundbite response. I do not believe in miracles but I do believe in the God of miracles. This is similar to many questions with regard to belief. For example, I have been baptised, but I do not believe in baptism. I do believe in the Trinity in whose name I was baptised.

I have puzzled over the definition of 'miracle'. It could be argued that I should have commenced with this. But this begs the question. Oliver Barclay in his CMF booklet[1] grapples with this problem. He gives a working definition that a miracle is a *wonder* due to God's *power* intended as a *sign*. Barclay then deals with the relation of miracles to natural law. This is at the heart of the problem and is one that has been debated for centuries. David Hume defined a miracle as a 'violation of the laws of nature or as a transgression of a law of nature by a particular volition of the Deity or by the interposition of some invisible agent.'[2] Professor

1. Barclay, O. R., *Science and Miracles*. Christian Medical Fellowship, Guidelines No. 90, London.
2. Huxley, *Hume*. MacMillan & Co., 1869.

T. H. Huxley, an otherwise great admirer of Hume, finds his views on miracles 'open to serious objection.' Huxley points out that the so-called laws of nature are nothing more than an observation on that which is. 'It is the sum of phenomena presented to our experience; the totality of events past, present, and to come. Every event must be taken to be a part of nature, until proof to the contrary is supplied. And such proof is, from the nature of the case impossible.' Huxley's own definition may be one of the best after all – 'The word "miracle" – *miraculum* – in its primitive and legitimate sense, simply means something wonderful.'

Hume wrote: 'It is a miracle that a dead man should come to life: because that has never been observed in any age or country.' Huxley again finds this view inconsistent. 'In truth, if a dead man did come to life, the fact would be evidence, not that any law of nature had been violated, but that those laws, even when they express the results of a very long and uniform experience, are necessarily based on incomplete knowledge, and are to be held only as grounds of more or less justifiable expectation.' Huxley goes on, in detail, to deal with claims of restoration of life and in the end concludes that such claims require irrefutable proof of death in a detailed medical fashion. He was anticipating a very contemporary debate.

Whilst we may learn from the way in which highly intelligent atheists may differ from each other, it can be seen that the ultimate question is not whether we 'believe in miracles of healing' or not. We do not even need to have unanimity as to the definition of our understanding of a miracle – whether in respect of healing from disease or otherwise. The difference with Hume, Huxley and likeminded people is in respect of belief in a transcendent God. The striking feature on this level is that Huxley shows impatience with Hume when he argues: 'Our most holy religion is founded on *Faith*, not reason . . . the Christian religion not only was first attended with miracles, but even at this day cannot be believed by any reasonable person without one. Mere reason is insufficient to convince us of its veracity: and whoever is moved by *Faith* to assent to it, which subverts all the principles of his understanding, and gives him a determination to believe what is most contrary to custom and experience.' I read these words with wonder over Hume's insight, even if there is more than a hint of irony. It is no surprise that Huxley confesses that because of these expressions and Hume's views on intelligent design and the nature of causation, he 'cannot but fall into perplexity.'

The way in which some of the great thinkers of the past have tried to grapple with these issues should challenge us. The level of thought and superficiality of the evidence in much of contemporary religious publications on the subject are in sharp contrast.

The believing Christian need not fear a confession of wonder when faced with the statement that 'great is the mystery of Godliness,' and that God's work in the creation of mankind and in his providence where he has the ultimate power and authority in the affairs of his creation, is one that should provoke us to worship in 'wonder, love and praise.'

Many aspects of the Christian faith show examples of the tension or paradox between what ought to be and what is experienced or practised. The classic one is that between faith and works. It is also shown in the field of healing, where we may find it difficult or impossible to reconcile what we say we believe with an experience which may appear to invalidate our profession. I believe it is better for us to acknowledge and accept such a tension, rather than be defeated or discouraged by it. This realisation should help us to retain some degree of humility on the subject. It will also prevent us from being over-dogmatic or too simplistic in our statements.

Recent developments in medical science show how contentious issues have to be re-visited. The methods of scientific research and their validation have been well-established for over a century. I have already attempted to show how people like Skrabanek have sought to de-bunk some fashionable crazes. However, these battles have to be constantly re-fought. Thus Professor David Colquhoun writes in the *British Medical Journal*,[3] criticising the failure of the royal medical colleges to address the resurgence of 'magic medicine.' The Department of Health itself 'refers the hard questions to the Prince of Wales' Foundation for Integrated Health.' When faced with requests for some sensible form of regulation of acupuncture and herbal and traditional Chinese medicine, Colquhoun observes: 'But you cannot start to think about a sensible form of regulation unless you first decide whether or not the thing you are trying to regulate is nonsense.' He deplores the 'evidence check: homeopathy' conducted by the House of Commons Science and Technology Select Committee in 2009, when all that needed to be said about 'medicine-free medicines' was said by Oliver Wendell Holmes in his 1842 essay, *Homeopathy and its Kindred Delusions.* But still the NHS spends £10 million annually on this.

I believe, in the same way, that Christians have to re-visit issues which have been debatable or even divisive in the past. This has been seen recently in basic aspects of the faith, such as the nature, extent and significance of Christ's atoning work on Calvary. The same applies to what we might regard as more peripheral topics of Christian belief and practice. Miracles of healing might be viewed as such. But yet I believe the debate is of relevance and significance – if only because some claims of miraculous healing are made, based on what is perceived as Christ's atoning work. If then the healing work is discredited there is the danger that the atonement suffers the same fate in the eyes of unbelievers or critics.

This is where I find it valuable to review some of the best contributions to the general debate on miraculous healing. One of the better ones is that from Henry Frost.[4] He begins his book by quoting five examples of healing in response to prayer. However,

---

3. Colquhoun, D., 'Secret Remedies: 100 years on', *BMJ*, 2009, 339:b5432.
4. Frost, H., *Miraculous Healing.* Evangelical Press, 1951, pp. 93, 118.

even here the diagnoses of sore throat, sea-sickness, nervous prostration and insanity, are hardly such as to lend themselves to falsification or satisfy the criteria which I have sought to establish for case histories. Frost, then proceeds to balance these with similar examples where God did not answer prayers for healing. He concludes his book with an account of the healing of his son from meningitis. But the evidence to support the diagnosis would not satisfy current medical criteria. He was writing at a time when bacteriological 'proof' was impossible and there is much in the history that is explicable on natural grounds. This is one reason why I find that the stance adopted by as godly a man as Frost, not entirely convincing. Faced with an acceptance that God is almighty and that God *can,* he has difficulty in distinguishing between genuine and unfounded claims. When he considers Christ's part in selecting those of his followers who would work miracles, he says this 'does not mean that He has never, from apostolic days to these, chosen others to heal sick saints, for facts, and even modern facts, are against such a conclusion.'

Frost is unequivocal when dealing with claims of resurrection – 'no saint, from the apostolic time to this, has ever raised anyone from the dead.'

The realm of the miraculous was an integral part of Paul's ministry – *'He simply would not have understood the presence of the Spirit that did not also include such manifestations of the Spirit that he termed "powers", which we translate "miracles"'.* Fee[5] goes on to express what I take to be the key to a Christian attitude to the entire problem – *'Paul's affirmations about miracles are not the statements of one who is trying to prove anything. That is, not only does he not point to miracles as grounds for accepting either his gospel or his ministry, but on the contrary he rejected such criteria as authenticating ministry of any kind. The cross, with the subsequent resurrection, and the present gift of the Spirit was all the authentication he ever appealed to. Those who need an occasional miracle to keep*

---

5. Fee, G. D., *God's Empowering Presence.* Paternoster, UK, 1995, p. 888.

their belief in God alive and those who feed on such "faith" by promoting the miraculous as authenticating their "gospel" also lie outside the Pauline perspective.'

The danger remains that when a Christian does re-examine the theory and practice of divine, miraculous, healing and becomes over critical in doing so, that a conflict is created between trust in an Almighty God as opposed to a God who is distant, uninvolved, and even incapable of taking a personal interest in any individual.

Each individual Christian must seek to find his or her position between the two extremes of irrational gullibility and an academic, rational position that is always in danger of degenerating into scepticism. Why cannot we have a faith that reflects our complete trust in the God who has loved us and given himself for us in the death of Christ; who one day will receive us into his presence with joy, whilst at the same time not expect God to intervene constantly in our lives at our behest to ensure our own comfort or protection? This should not entail that we hold views where we expect God to heal us at our request and especially when this is linked with some formulaic type of healing worship or incantation. These simplistic and exaggerated views and practices can do nothing but bring discredit on the true gospel of the Christian life and faith.

The greatest good for me is that I should know God as he has revealed himself in Jesus Christ. God's unique and supreme gift is Himself. In his grace and mercy he may and does bestow countless other gifts, but these are as nothing compared with himself – in fact, they are a distraction if they should either lessen my longing for the Giver or be a substitute for the ultimate goal to see and worship God forever.